GEORGE BEASLEY'S BETTER ANGEL

Also by Jean Davies Okimoto

NOVELS
The Love Ceiling
Walter's Muse
The Reinvention of Albert Paugh
George Beasley's Better Angel

NON-FICTION
Boomerang Kids:
How to live with Adult Children
Who Return Home

PLAYS
Hum it Again, Jeremy
Uncle Hideki
Uncle Hideki and the Empty Nest
The Reinvention of Albert Paugh
Winston of Churchill
Turn the Corner, George!

YOUNG ADULT AND MIDDLE GRADE NOVELS
Jason's Women
Molly by Any other Name
To Jaykae: Life Stinx
The Elcipse of Moonbeam Dawson
Talent Night
My Mother Is Not Married to My Father
It's Just Too Much
Norman Schnurman, Average Person
Take a Chance, Gramps
Maya and the Cotton Candy Boy
Who Did it Jenny Lake?

PICTURE BOOKS
Blumpoe the Grumpoe Meet Arnold the Cat
A Place for Grace
Dear Ichiro
No Dear Not Here
Winston of Churchill
Five Famous Mice Meet Winston of Churchill
The White Swan Express
Jake and Emma's Island Getaway

George Beasley's Better Angel

BY JEAN DAVIES OKIMOTO

ENDICOTT
and HUGH
BOOKS

This is a work of fiction. All the characters and events portrayed in this novel are either fictitious or are used fictitiously, with the exception of those names used with permission.

Okimoto, Jean Davies. George Beasley's Better Angel: a novel / by Jean Davies Okimoto.

Brown, Leslie "When Body Washed Ashore, a Woman Came Back Home, Daughter Says" Vashon-Maury Beachcomber, Feb. 27, 2013

pages ; cm

ISBN: 978-0-9993646-6-6 (paperback) ISBN: 978-0-9993646-7-3 (ebook)

1. Aging—Fiction. 2. Widowed-divorced men—Fiction. 3. Man-woman relationships—Fiction. 4. Vashon Island (Wash.)—Fiction. 5. Love stories, American. I. Title.

Book and cover design: Masha Shubin
Cover art: Sandy Trammell

Printed in the United States of America

10 9 8 7 6 5 4 3 2

For Joe, Amy and Katie

CONTENTS

Three things in human life are important:
the first is to be kind; the second is to be kind;
and the third is to be kind.

-Henry James

EDDIE

I T WAS A TERRIBLE, COMPLETELY NASTY MORNING THAT only added to my coffin of gloom. Another nail in it. The weather report had predicted it, but I didn't believe it. Not that I thought it was fake news or that we had a President who would scribble on the forecast with a Sharpie. It's just that it changed so often you couldn't count on what they'd forecasted. And people always said the same old thing, "Don't like the weather? Wait five minutes and it will change." Same old. Same old. But a lot of truth to that. Especially around here.

They'd predicted heavy rain with wind gusts up to fifty miles an hour, enough to cause a lot of damage, and maybe I ignored it like that Harry Truman guy (not the President, but the guy with the same name who wouldn't evacuate when Mt. St. Helens blew up and he got killed in a mud side). I wondered if a death like that would be so fast it would be painless. Maybe the giant, gloppy avalanche of mud would smash over you and bury you before you even knew what happened.

I was in the kitchen thinking about Harry Truman's death when the power went out. No surprise. Especially in a wind like this. But at least the coffee had finished brewing. At the exact second Mr. Coffee made that little bubbley hiss when the last drop plopped in the pot—zap!—off went the coffee maker and with it all the lights. Bess would have said, "What timing! The coffee gods are with us, George." And she'd laugh, celebrating the good luck of it all. Gratitude. That was something Bess was good at—but me, not so much. Actually not much at all. If I were going to be graded, I'd get an F or, at best, a D in Gratitude. People who can feel it are supposed to be happier. And I have tried to conjure up some gratitude, making an effort to focus on things such as birds, or the sun, or the beauty of the earth. But then I think of the bird poo all over my truck, the awful sunburn I got when Bess and I went to Hawaii, and how climate change is destroying the earth. I didn't used to be like this, but it's like a lot of things that I used to be, for instance: young. I used to be young. I caught my reflection in the shiny metal side of Mr. Coffee as I pulled out the pot. The stubble made me look like an old homeless dude, and my Schnauzery eyebrows looked like little McDonald arches made of grungy, gray scraggly bushes. Honestly, what had she ever seen in me?

Hopefully, the coffee would still be warm by the time Eddie got here. We had coffee every morning. Coffee with Eddie was a habit like getting out of bed, doing your bathroom business and brushing your teeth. Although the truth is, I don't always want to get out of bed. If it weren't for the chickens maybe I wouldn't. Even though we have automatic water and feed dispensers, I still have to go out and fill the dispensers. Bess loved the chickens. Getting them was her idea and when I suggested she get a bigger dispenser so she wouldn't have to go out every morning, she gave me a look like, "How could you not get how I feel about them? Don't you understand the pleasure I get from greeting them every morning?" She especially loved feeding them table scraps: lettuce and other greens, melon and cantaloupe rinds, and corn cobs—they'd peck on those suckers all day. She'd bring the scraps out every morning and they'd be at the gate of the pen waiting for her, clucking softly. They had a relationship. I know they're mad at me because I don't bring them scraps. Scraps are just a bridge too far—water and chicken feed, that's it for me. The basics. I have to admit I had thought about eating the chickens, but then I'd have to deal with the feathers. But worse than that would be the guilt. I know how Bess would feel, what she would say—and I couldn't stand that.

Out in the yard the wind was whipping the trees around, firs hundreds of feet tall were being buffeted and bent by the force of the wind. They looked like they could be stalks of long dark grass in a yard that needed mowing, like mine. And branches of all sizes had broken off and were careening every which way across the yard, making it even more of a mess. At the end of our road a stand of alders looked ruined. They had been stripped of so many branches that down the hill I could see a slice of the usually placid cove churning in a frenzy pounding Baker's Beach. And I could hear Bess, "Hey, isn't that great—we now have view property!" Her take on a disappointment, the way she'd spin it to flip it to the positive never failed to warm me. That was Bess, sunshine on a cloudy day, like that old song, "I've got sunshine on a cloudy day /

When it's cold outside I've got the month of May / My Girl—talkin' 'bout my girl." Was it the Temptations, or maybe the Platters—one of those sixties doo-wop groups? Not that it matters if I remember. Who cares? And to be precise, she wasn't my girl back then. I just dreamed about her. Unattainable, like she is now all these years later. I tried to bring her close and made an effort to look through the ruined trees to focus on the cove the way she would. But I couldn't get there. I couldn't see the good in any of it and it only made me feel more alone. Alone is different for me than being lonely, which had been my default setting for most of my early life. I was used to that like chronic lower back pain that you try to ignore and learn to live with. No, feeling alone was more than a dull ache—it was bleak and dismal, completely bereft. And along with it there were little pinpricks of fear.

Next to the house, the trees bent and the wind battered their bigger remaining branches. Maybe a huge limb, or the entire tree would fall on the house. I had the thought that it might not be a bad way to go. Getting demolished by my house. When a guy died mountain climbing people would say, he died doing what he loved. But what would they say about a guy who sits around doing nothing and gets offed by his house? The whole roof would have to collapse very forcefully on top of me to completely do the job. I wouldn't want to end up being a vegetable like Eddie's neighbor. The guy had a stroke, but it didn't do him in, his brain just turned to mush. No thank you. It should be all or nothing. As I was thinking about that, I got a text from Eddie.

George—I got something important to tell you.
Should be there in about fifteen minutes. Lord
willin' and the creek don't rise. ha ha

That was odd. Eddie usually just shows up. Never
calls first and I never lock my doors so he comes right
in. And while he's here he goes in the chicken coop
and gets the eggs because I don't like to do that part. I
don't like going in the coop at all. Especially if it's been
a while since I'd cleaned it out and put down fresh
straw. Although I've discovered if you wait a while the
chicken shit has dried up so it's not as bad as when it's
fresh. Fresh chicken shit is not appealing. But none of
it bothered Bess, which I found remarkable.

I didn't like Eddie when I first met him on the
ferry. We were both working at Boeing so we decided
to carpool. Was that thirty years ago? Oh, who cares
when—I just didn't dig the guy. He's a skittery, jumpy
type like a squirrel. Actually, his looks remind me of
Mr. Peanut, the guy who used to be on Planter's Pea-
nuts, without the top hat, of course. And he talked too
much, which got on my nerves. But over the years I
got used to it. It was like when you have a refrigerator
that hums and after a while you just don't hear it. And
actually I found I didn't mind how much Eddie talked
because it just meant if I didn't feel like talking in the
morning, I didn't have to. Although we did have our
disagreements, usually on the commute back to the
island. He was a NASCAR fan and I don't consider
anything to do with a machine a sport. He argued
that the car was just another piece of sports equipment
like bobsleds, skates, skis, or snowboards which were

all Olympic sports. It was a stupid comparison and we went round and round and finally dropped it.

I was checking my phone to see how much battery I had left when I heard a resounding crack and then glass shattering. Great. Something to make the house more of a wreck. But I couldn't see any damage, at least in the living room or the kitchen. A window must have broken somewhere. I knew I should check it out-—not that I really cared. But Bess would want me to. So I started inspecting the roof and windows around the main floor. Without Bess I hadn't been looking closely at anything. I've been operating detached from most things, fuzzy and in a fog. But as I looked for damage, I became aware of the actual state of the kitchen. Dishes piled in the sink, rotting food stuck to pans, empty pizza boxes and take-out cartons covering the counters, my clothes draped over chairs and on the floor, dried mud caked near the door—Bess would wonder what the hell had happened. Well, we both know what happened.

There were two bedrooms and a bathroom on the main floor, and they were just as much of a mess, but structurally intact. Whatever glass shattering I'd heard must have been in the basement—I rarely went down there. It had been her domain. There was a bedroom and bath which took up half the daylight basement. A basement of her own, we'd joked. The closets were filled with her summer clothes in winter, and winter clothes in summer and a bunch she referred to as her thin clothes. The ones she'd kept for decades, or bought on sale, as an incentive to fit into them someday.

When I opened the door at the bottom of the

stairs, I saw water spreading all across the floor. It didn't take a genius to see what had happened. A huge limb had busted the south window and was sticking into the room like something that had flown off a logging truck. Tiny pebbles of splintered glass decorated the shelves like confetti, and larger jagged shards lay all across the floor from the window to the bed. I closed the door and started back up the stairs. Feeding the chickens was about all I could manage in a day, and there was no way in hell that I could even begin to take on the friggin' basement. Screw it.

"George! I gotta talk to you George!"

"I'm down here! Be right up!" I sloshed through the water and my slippers got soaked. They were nice slippers, chocolate brown with cozy fleece stuff inside. They'd been a birthday present from Bess and there were a lot of days I didn't bother changing into shoes. I hoped they weren't wrecked. Then Eddie yelled again. He is never known for patience, but he did sound urgent. My slippers squished as I went up the stairs and the minute I got to the top, he was right in my face.

"I couldn't wait to see you today."

He was grinning. That threw me. "Everything okay?"

"I'm great. Never better."

"I gotta change my slippers."

Eddie looked at my feet. "They're wet."

"You're very observant."

"How'd they get wet?"

"The basement. I'll be right back." I went to the bedroom, took off my slippers and put them next to the baseboard heater. There were a bunch of socks on the floor so I got a couple, pulled them on and then my boots and went back to Eddie. "I'll get your coffee. It finished right before we lost power. Not hot, but still a little warm, I hope." I refilled my cup and got him one. "So everything's okay over at your place?"

"Branches all over, but no damage. Just waiting for the power to come back." He sipped his coffee, and paused, looking down at the cup. "Not exactly hot."

"I told you."

"I'm not complaining. Listen, I couldn't wait to get here this morning."

"You stop by every morning."

Eddie took off his rain parka and threw it over a chair. "I had a dream last night."

"That's it? Listen, Eddie I got a big damn mess in the basement. A huge limb went through the window, the floor's flooded and there's glass all over the place." Just thinking about it overwhelmed me again and I plopped down on the wing chair next to the fireplace. The chair was covered in orange and brown plaid. We'd gotten it years ago at a big furniture closeout at Macy's warehouse. One of the arms had a little stuffing sticking out from a seam that Bess had planned on fixing and I'd been picking at it, not even knowing I was doing it, and now the hole was the size of a baby's fist. I sipped my coffee and tried to poke the stuffing back in the hole. It was a project that seemed manageable.

Eddie pulled up the ottoman and sat down right in front of me. "We were on the front page of the *Beachcomber*!"

I nodded and poked at the chair stuffing.

"A headline, our names in big letters—George Beasley and Eddie Mahoney—it was a big story."

"What'd we do? Rob the pharmacy?"

"Nothing like that. We had a business—and people came to us from miles around. But I didn't know what kind of a business because I woke up."

"That's it?"

"No, listen. See, it gave me this great idea. I've been awake since three a.m." Eddie pulled a sheet of paper from his shirt pocket and unfolded it. "I got this done before we lost power and I printed it out."

"Mind telling me what it is, Eddie?"

"Airbnb!" He jumped up, spilling his coffee. "Opps. Sorry about that." He stuffed the paper back in his pocket, scurried to the kitchen, got a rag and frantically started wiping the floor.

"Don't worry about that."

"I got it. Didn't spill that much." He looked at the floor, satisfied and stood up. "So, here's the deal— we'll rent out the room in your basement." He waited a minute to let the news sink in, then took the rag back to the kitchen and returned to sit on the ottoman facing me. Eddie leaned forward with his hands on his knees and paused, like he was about to announce the winner of the lottery, then whispered, "We're going to make a lot of money, George."

"I don't get the *we* here. How's it our business when it's my house."

"I don't have a house."

"So, it's finally done?"

"Yep. I moved out today." He motioned toward the door, "My stuff's out in my truck. Marlene bought me out, so she has the house and the dog, too." Eddie looked down at the floor. "I'm going to miss her, George."

"Marlene?"

"Not her. The dog. I didn't have to lose Peaches when we first split up."

I sipped my coffee. "Never seemed like you really split up."

"Living in the attic was always just temporary."

"For three years?"

"Well, we had to wait for her to buy me out and—"

"For her father to kick the bucket, you mean."

"You could put it that way. She knew he'd leave her the money."

"I saw his obituary in the *Beachcomber* last week." I felt more than a little bitter when I read it. Marlene's father was a nasty piece of work. A contractor who was always stiffing his subs, everyone knew it. How fair was that, when a jerk like that lived such a long life and a saint like Bess never even made it to seventy?"

"He was 102. We didn't think he'd last past 100." Eddie looked out the window. "You know, lately, whenever somebody dies I can't help wondering about how much time I've got. And then I always start thinking about what I want to do before I die. Like a bucket list, you know. Do you have one, George?"

"A what?"

"A bucket list."

I didn't say anything. I hadn't needed one. I had everything I wanted. I had Bess. I poked more stuffing in the hole—I hadn't realized that I had started pulling it out again. "I didn't see the point of a bucket list, but Bess wanted to make one for both of us. But then it was too late." I poked at the stuffing. "I can't seem to get beyond it."

"Bess died two years ago, George."

"Tell me something I don't know."

"I didn't mean to sound harsh."

"Most days I think she's still here." I didn't tell him that when I realize she's not, I get hit with a wave of the emptiness all over again and it flattens me and then I don't see the point. The point of anything.

"Well, she is still here … as they say, in your heart." Eddie leaned forward and patted my arm. "But you've gotta face it, she's gone. Time to move on. Turn the corner."

Eddie was a fine one to talk. He lived in the attic for three years and maybe it was partly because of the money, but I knew he couldn't face the fact that his marriage was over. Eddie always thinks things are going to work out. It's different from the way Bess could find the good in things. She didn't pretend the bad wasn't there, she acknowledged it and moved through it—and then looked ahead and found some nugget of good or hope. Eddie just blocked out the bad, as if it wasn't even there—he couldn't face things. He was a champion denier, and here *he* was telling me that I have to face that Bess is gone. *Really?*

I didn't feel like arguing and telling him that he was a fine one to talk. What good would it do? Besides, that flooded mess in the basement was lurking right under me and that was what I needed to face. I closed my eyes and leaned back, trying to muster the where-withal to go deal with it. But I didn't feel like moving. I felt like my butt was glued to the chair with Gorilla Glue or one of those industrial adhesives they use to make airplanes. I opened one eye and looked at Eddie.

Maybe he could help motivate me to deal with the basement. But it was more than that. Because deep down, I had to admit that I knew Eddie was right. I did need to get a life. A life without Bess. I sighed and sat up. "I know I have to face it. It's just that I can't believe she's gone."

"What's not to believe. We saw her in the casket. She looked good, too. I mean, for a dead person."

"She did. But I know she wouldn't like how they fixed her hair."

"I thought there was something different—besides being dead and all. But I couldn't put my finger on it."

"It was the bangs. They combed her hair to make bangs. To cover the bump she got when she keeled over."

I hadn't had any part in the service for Bess or any of the arrangements. I was practically catatonic at the time, so her friends Annabel, Jackie, June and Carol took over. They met at our house and tried hard to include me, but I just sat in the plaid chair like a vegetable. They asked about her burial wishes, and if there were any other family members who should be consulted—but it was just me and I couldn't remember or deal with anything. The only other family was Bess's cousin Susan, who was like a sister to her and had died of pancreatic cancer fifteen years ago, and Susan's daughter and her family were living in London. Bess's friends kept asking me what I wanted, but all I wanted was Bess not to be dead.

As they discussed it, at first they were in agreement that cremation was bad for the environment. But then they went round and round because they had different opinions. Annabel thought there should be a green burial where they put the dead person in a shroud. She said there's no embalming with toxic chemicals or a casket with any metal and the shroud could be made out of anything that was biodegradable. She suggested that wrapping Bess in a cotton quilt like they raffle off at Strawberry Festival would be perfect for her. But Jackie said there weren't any green burial cemeteries on the island yet, and you couldn't just find some land and dig a hole. It had to be a legal green burial cemetery. She reminded them that if George wanted to visit the grave he'd have to go off island. I think they forgot I was sitting there. Jackie voted for a new kind of burial called terramation and explained they put the dead person in a sealed container with some organic stuff like straw or sawdust and put in oxygen and after a few months the body turns into soil. It becomes this very organic dirt, she said, and then George could do what he wanted with it, such as putting the soil in the yard and creating a special garden. In fact, they could all come over and help George plant something. They started discussing what kind of plants should be there, such as mostly native plants and some rhododendrons, our state flower.

I felt like I was watching them from another planet and then I really felt that way because June said the best thing to do for the environment was the very latest method of body disposal, alkaline hydrolysis where the body goes in a machine that turns it into liquid and then it's washed down the drain. Carol didn't like the sound of that—she was the most traditional of Bess's friends and she had strong feelings that viewing the body helped with grieving and accepting the loss. She looked over at me and asked me what I thought. I sat there staring at them and couldn't speak. I'm sure I looked shell-shocked, so Carol said they should leave. I don't know how any of it eventually got decided. My guess is that Annabel, Jackie and June probably kept arguing about the best green method and Carol took charge so the service ended up at the funeral home with Bess in an open casket.

Eddie stared out the window, shaking his head. "What a shock that was, heart attack like that."

"Tell me something I don't know," I snapped.

Then he looked at me and jumped up, took the paper from his pocket and waved it. "Here's something you don't know! It's all about our Airbnb—"

"What's with the *our*?" I went to the kitchen and put my cup on the counter. "Listen Eddie, I got to get back to the basement and clean up that mess."

"I'll help you."

"Okay—I wouldn't mind a hand." Bess used to say many hands makes light work. She was a hard worker, too, which had surprised me early on. I never thought such a beautiful girl would take on the things she did. She was fearless. She'd tackle any job. The house had been pretty run-down when we bought it from some trust-fund hippies who'd let it go to pot, literally. And the two of us did all the work ourselves: new bathroom fixtures, new floor, double pane windows, but not the basement windows. I headed down there, wondering if we'd put double pane if that tree would have busted through.

"Jeez. This is a mess." Edie stopped in the doorway, staring at the glass and the water all over the floor.

"What'd I tell you."

"Let's get the glass up first. Got any gloves? Where's the mop?"

"In the storage room." I pointed to the door next to the bathroom. "Oh, wait. I forgot. I've got a shop vac and it can suck up water. You just take out the paper bag."

"That'll be faster. Where is it?"

"In the storage room."

"I know. But *where* in the storage room? It's a mess in there."

"I'm well aware of that, Eddie. Did you have to point that out?"

"I don't want to plow through all that stuff if you know where it is."

"It might be a mess, but I do know where everything is."

"Fine. So where is it?"

"In the corner next to the leaf blower," I said, taking a chance it might actually be there.

Eddie went in the storage room and came back a few minutes later.

"Is there somethin' wrong with the vac?" I asked him.

"There's no power."

"Oh right, I forgot."

"I've got bad news." Eddie motioned to me. "Take a look in here," he walked over to the bathroom and opened the door. "It's the toilet, George. True, some of that water came in when that limb broke through, but most of it's 'cause you've got a leak somewhere and I'm almost positive it's the septic"

"Oh shit."

"You got that right," Eddie laughed.

"I don't think that's funny."

"Fine. Whatever." Eddie shrugged and looked around. "Where's the water turn-off? They're usually somewhere in the basement."

"Next to the hot water heater."

"I'll do it—you better call the septic people. I'll get my chain saw from my truck and I can get the limb outa here in no time. Then we can fix the window later."

"You don't have to do that—I can take care of it."

Eddie grinned. "The sooner we fix up this place the sooner we can open our Airbnb. Go call the septic people, George. I got this. And then I can show you what I found on the internet—this business is gonna be great. I guarantee it."

"You sound like that guy selling suits on TV," I muttered as I went up the stairs. Eddie was putting up a brave front. Knowing him, he probably never planned for the day that Marlene would buy him out of the house. In fact, if they never got around to actually divorcing I could see him living in the attic forever. But now that it's finally a done deal, he probably doesn't have a clue about where to live.

I went back to the living room and got my phone. Plenty of battery left, at least that's one good thing, I thought, as I called Island Septic. But they didn't pick up. All I got was a recording that said they were booked until the next week, but they did give the number of another septic service. I'd never heard of it, but I didn't think they would recommend some fly-by-night scammer. So I called the number, and the guy answered right away. He spoke with an accent that I couldn't quite place, but I could understand him and he said he'd come Monday. That seemed pretty quick, so he obviously wasn't that busy, which worried me. And I worried if it would cost an arm and a leg. Anything with a septic is a big friggin' deal.

The wind had died down quite a bit and I wondered when we'd get the power back. We'd never gotten a generator like a lot of folks on the island. Bess always thought it was an adventure when the power went out. We'd make a fire, light dozens of candles and hold hands, or cuddle or ... I felt my throat swell up, thinking of the times we made love in front of the fire. And sometimes we'd played cards by candlelight, too. Sometimes we'd sing. Bess had a beautiful voice. She was part of a singing group that worked with hospice people and sang for people when they were dying. But no one sang for her. How shabby was that?

I went to the coffee pot and decided I'd rather have cold coffee than none and poured another cup. In a few minutes I heard Eddie's chain saw. It was nice of him to help. When Eddie was done with the tree limb, I'd just tell him he could stay here until he figured out where to live. We'd been friends for so long, I didn't know why Eddie thought he had to pretend it was about some business deal.

I checked the Puget Sound Energy app on my phone. I like the app, it shows your location and the time they estimate the power will be back. Although they often err on the optimistic side. Then I heard the chain saw stop and in a few minutes Eddie came up the stairs.

"Got the limb taken care of—and I can get the water vacuumed up when the power's back."

"Thanks, Eddie." I looked at my phone. "PSE says it'll be on around two this afternoon."

"Hope they're right, it's freezing in here. How 'bout I make a fire."

"I can make the fire. Listen Eddie, I've got plenty of room, you can just crash here until you decide what's next for you."

"Thanks, George. I appreciate that, I really do. But I know what's next—it's our Airbnb," he grinned. "And don't worry. I won't be just crashing here—I'll pay rent for living here while we run the business. This is strictly business—I'm not a freeloader in spite of what Marlene says."

"She did bad-mouth you quite a bit."

"Yeah, well that's all in the past now." Eddie pulled the paper from his pocket again. "Oh, and when I collect the eggs, I'll bring them in so we can have them here."

"Fine. Whatever." Eddie had been collecting the eggs every day for the past two years. It started when he came over after the memorial service and smelled something awful coming from the coop. He went in and saw the eggs had piled up, dropped out of the nests, and broken all over the floor and were rotting. He said he'd be happy to get them for me when he came every morning for coffee. But I didn't want them. I didn't feel like eating eggs—I didn't have an appetite for anything then, not just eggs. So Eddie had been taking them home ever since.

He studied the paper and looked up. "We'll have to figure out what kind of pillows to get."

"What are you talking about?"

"It says you get nice reviews if you have nice accoutrements."

"Nice accoutrements!" I put down my coffee cup. "Look at this place—it's gone to hell—like me. Face it, it's a dump now. Didn't used to be, but ever since—"

"We just need to fix it up a little. You gotta broom, don't ya?"

I was too tired to argue and half-heartedly motioned to the closet by the basement stairs. Eddie put the paper back in his pocket and charged over to the closet, got the broom and began running all over the place swinging the broom around, swatting the cobwebs.

"What are you doing, Eddie?" I started to cough.

"Cleaning up. No one wants to stay in these cobwebs. It's not a selling point."

"I don't believe this." I coughed so much, I had to get some water.

Eddie leaned on the broom and pulled out the paper again. Then he went over to me as I was gulping water and waved the paper in front of my face. "Just read this. That's all I ask. Just read it."

"Oh all right, what the hell." I grabbed the paper from Eddie. It would be easier than arguing with him. I went back to the chair, sat down, took one look at the paper and put it down. "Damn."

"What's wrong?"

"I don't know where I put my glasses." I fumbled around the coffee table looking under the old *Beachcombers* and all the piles of mail.

Eddie spotted them on the kitchen counter and brought them to me. "See, you need me."

I coughed. "Yeah, to stir up all the dust." I put on my glasses and started to read, while Eddie continued swinging the broom at the cobwebs. When he was satisfied he'd gotten most of them—although I wasn't convinced because he doesn't see that well—he went to the broom closet, found the dustpan and began sweeping the floor.

After a few minutes, I put down the paper and took off my glasses. "I don't want people in my basement who might mess up my stuff. Like my fishing rod."

Eddie stopped sweeping. "What are you talking about?"

"That time you borrowed it when your cousin came and the tip got broken."

"That was five years ago and I fixed it."

"It was never right again."

"I can't believe you're holding a grudge, George."

"I'm not. I just don't like people borrowing my stuff, that's all." I put my glasses back on and as I read about it, first skimming and then more carefully, I did have to admit this Airbnb thing actually did seem like it could be a legitimate business. Maybe it wasn't just some excuse to stay here. But Eddie had a lousy track record. He was a dreamer—I can't begin to count all the schemes Eddie would talk about when we rode to work together. He seemed to get a lot of pleasure from thinking up all his great plans, and maybe that was enough because he never actually did anything about them. The only one he actually tried to pursue was his lawn chair balloon festival. Eddie was inspired by the guy in California who went up in the air in a lawn chair tied with a bunch of helium balloons. The guy used a BB gun to shoot out the balloons to slowly make his descent. Eddie found this feat thrilling and was convinced many people would want to do this. "Going up in the sky in your own lawn chair, it would be amazing!" He went on and on about it and, unusual for him, put a lot of thought into the details. He even bought a helium tank on amazon for $47. In his vision for the festival, it would be held at Ober Park and there would be an entry fee for each person who wanted to go up in a lawn chair—they'd have to supply their own chair—and he'd purchase the balloons with the entry fees. And the spectators would have to pay, too, like they did to watch the Sheepdog Trials which had been very popular. He was convinced his festival would go on year after year, like the island's annual Strawberry Festival. He created a draft of a press release for the *Beachcomber* that would announce the First Annual Vashon Island Lawn Chair Balloon Festival. In big caps at the top, Eddie wrote that it would be patterned after the Albuquerque International Balloon Fiesta. He was convinced mentioning the Albuquerque festival would create excitement and even attract people from off-island just like the Strawberry Festival, and the Sheepdog Trials did when they used to have them. "It's important to market widely, George. So I'll be sending the press release both to the *Seattle Times* and the *Tacoma News Tribune*." Eddie spent days on the press release, obsessing about it and reading different versions aloud to me as we sat in the truck on the ferry. When he thought it was ready, all he needed to do was add the date and time. He thought there'd probably be some kind of a permit required by the park department and when he called them to reserve the park, they immediately had safety concerns and when they mentioned liability and insurance, well, that was the end of it. I wanted to suggest to Eddie that he should have called the park department first before he wrote the press release and bought the helium tank, but I thought better of it because he was very upset. On the ferry, he just sat in the truck looking out at the water not saying a word. I thought of trying to jolly him up with a little joke, saying the First Annual Vashon Island Lawn Chair Balloon Festival never got off the ground, but I thought better of that, too.

I put the paper down and looked up at Eddie. "It says here in the summer you could make $500 a week. That can't be right."

"It's true. Believe me."

"You really think someone would pay $70 a night to sleep in my basement?"

"Absolutely."

"Right." And then I blurted, "And you were sure people would pay to be in the Vashon Island Lawn Chair Balloon Festival."

"Did you really have to bring that up, George?"

"I never said a word at the time if you remember. And I could have. I could have said it collapsed, or fizzled, or the air went out of it."

"That's not funny."

"I knew you wouldn't think it was funny, that's why I didn't say it."

"Listen, if you don't believe it, we should talk to

Lottie. Her beach house is an Airbnb. We should invite her for a drink and ask her all about it."

"Lottie hates me."

"Lottie?" Eddie was surprised.

"It's true."

"Lottie's a nice woman, that can't be right."

"Believe me, it is. When she brought over a casserole, I took the opportunity to tell her how terrible her dog is."

"Max? He's a nice dog. Besides, that was two years ago."

"Bess's chickens don't think so. I told Lottie to keep him the hell outa my yard."

"I'm sure she knew you weren't yourself, George." Eddie started sweeping in front of the fireplace, then he stopped. "Why is it when your wife dies you get casseroles, but when your wife dumps you, do you get anything? No. Nothing. Nada." He started sweeping again. "It doesn't seem right."

"Bess always told her divorced friends there are two sides to every divorce—the woman's and the shithead's."

"Well, I coulda used some casseroles." Eddie got the dustpan and swept the dirt into it. "Listen, I'm sure Lottie's over it. That was two years ago."

I wasn't convinced. "People get very upset if you insult their dogs. Animals are family members and you never forget if someone criticizes them. But that's not the whole thing with me and Lottie, anyway."

"What else?"

I checked my phone again to see if they'd updated the time when we'd get the power back on. "Now PSE says it won't come back until 5:00."

"What d'ya mean that's not the whole thing with you and Lottie?"

It was about a year after Bess died. It was like I could hear her telling me I had to get out and make a life for myself. I could often hear her telling me stuff, like she was with me. But then it would hit me that she was gone and I'd be crushed again. But this time I tried to please her and do what she wanted, so I decided to try a couple of things, but they were both terrible. Complete disasters. I didn't want to talk about it. "It is cold in here. I'll go get some wood." I went out the back door to the side of the garage where the wood was stacked and brought in a few logs. The stack was getting low, which meant that I'd have to get a cord and start splitting it. Just thinking about it was another thing that was overwhelming.

"What happened with Lottie, George?"

"What?"

"I said, 'what happened with Lottie?'"

I opened the fire screen and grabbed a few old *Beachcombers* and crumpled them up and placed them over the grate. "I forgot kindling." I went back out to the woodpile and picked up a bunch of kindling from a box by the edge of the pile. When I brought in the kindling, Eddie asked me again about Lottie.

"What happened with—"

"Jeez—you're like a terrier with a bone." I knelt in front of the fireplace and arranged the kindling. "Oh, I suppose I better tell you." I lit the paper and when the kindling caught, I lay the logs on top and closed the screen. "It happened when I saw there was a new church starting up–"

"What church? I didn't know you went to church."

"I saw a flyer about it, or maybe it was a poster at Cafe Luna. Doesn't matter. Anyway, it's called the Church of the Holy Tree."

"Another Catholic church?" Eddie was surprised. "We already got one."

"Not Holy See. Holy *Tree*. Church of the Holy Tree, it's in a yurt in Paradise Valley. The sign said—come to think of it, it was at Cafe Luna. Anyway, the sign said they were having a field trip trying to get new members."

Eddie went to the kitchen and looked around. "I guess there's no point in cleaning this up until the power's back on. The water's probably gotten cold." He went back and sat across from me. "So what does this have to do with Lottie?"

"She went on the field trip and I sat next to her in the van."

"Where'd you go?"

I got the poker, opened the screen and prodded one of the logs. "This isn't catching that well, the logs must not be that dry."

"Where'd you go on the field trip, George?"

"To Seattle. To a pot shop. It was before we had pot shops on the island. The church people were interested in learning about the health benefits of weed. And I don't sleep well and I thought it might help. So I bought these brownies. Edibles they call them." I poked the logs some more, then added more kindling. "I got hungry walking back to the van and ate the brownies. I lost track and ate the whole package. And when I sat in the van and looked all around, the sun made all these pretty colors and I told Lottie her wrinkles looked like magical etchings, and the lines over her lips looked like little dancing stick figures. I tried to describe what I was seeing, because it all looked so pretty and interesting. At least that's how I remember it."

"Oh George." Eddie shook his head.

"Then I said the little hair on her chin looked like a golden thread and I took her hand to kiss it and I slobbered all over it."

"At least you didn't throw up."

"Yeah, I guess that's something."

Eddie went to the kitchen and got the broom and started sweeping the dried mud that was caked by the front door. "Did you ever apologize?"

"I was giggling a lot in the van, so no. Not then."

"What about later?"

"When I see Lottie at Thriftway, she whips her cart around and runs down another aisle." I opened the screen and put another log on the fire. "If Bess were here, she'd tell me how to fix it."

Eddie stopped sweeping. "Try apologizing."

I watched the log to see if it caught and thought about how Bess approached things. She didn't exactly boss me around—she was just a very practical and organized person. She had to be ever since she was a kid, her mother was so out of it. I turned to Eddie. "You know Bess was a good problem-solver. And she had lists for everything. I miss those lists."

Eddie put the broom down and walked over to me. "I'll tell you what to do. Here's a list. When Lottie comes over, number one: tell her you're sorry that you got stoned on the church field trip. Number two: tell her she's pretty. Women like that."

I sat back down on the plaid chair. "I don't know, Eddie."

"When I invite her for a drink, I'll mention that you've been feeling terrible about the field trip. That'll pave the way." Eddie went back to the broom and began sweeping again. "What happened about her dog? Any more problems?"

"She keeps Max in at night, so he hasn't been around."

"Good. So all you have to do is say you're sorry about getting stoned."

MARTHA JANE

THE NIGHTS HAVE ALWAYS BEEN THE WORST. I READ somewhere that after your spouse dies you should sleep on their side of the bed, because if you're on your side and you reach for them it makes it worse. I tried this and it didn't help. And having another person in the house didn't help either. Eddie snored. The rumble was rhythmic with a cadence that might have actually aided my sleep like waves rolling onto the shore, except that each rumble was tapped off with a high pitched fluttery whistle. It sounded like the trill of an obnoxious bird coming from the next bedroom, one that you'd like to strangle. I was going to need earplugs or I'd never get any sleep.

Eddie, who had slept great, was up early. He looked different; he must have cleaned up a little and shaved. The white and grayish bristles were gone and he smelled different—after shave, I suppose; I'd seen a bottle of Old Spice in the bathroom. When I went out to feed the chickens, he was busy cleaning the kitchen. I've never been a morning person, but when I haven't slept everything pisses me off. Eddie was chipper and bopping around the kitchen which was completely irritating. By the time I came back he had coffee ready and handed me a cup. He was obviously trying very hard to be useful.

"Thanks," I said, making a great effort to be civil. I took the coffee and sat at the table.

"I called Lottie."

"You what?"

"Lottie. I called her, like we talked about."

"I didn't say to do it," I snapped. "When? It's too early to call people."

"When I went out to collect the eggs I saw the light on over at her place. She was up."

"You don't know that. Some people leave lights on and they're asleep."

"Well, she was awake and she said she'd be happy to tell us about her Airbnb." Eddie sounded very cheerful as he brought his coffee over and sat across from me.

"You really asked her to come here ... to my house?"

"Of course. I told her we are going to open an Airbnb and we wanted to pick her brains."

"*Thinking* about it, Eddie—we're only thinking about this Airbnb. Nothing's been decided."

"Believe me, when you learn about it, you'll want to do it."

"Pfft," I scoffed, but then Eddie looked hurt so I just sighed and drank my coffee. I thought I'd probably have to humor him until he got this idea out of his system. Giving Eddie a place to crash was something I felt obligated to do, like feeding the chickens. Although I didn't have the option of killing and eating him ...oh Jeez ... I gripped my coffee and just shook my head ... I'm losing it ... I gotta go back to bed and start over.

"We should clean up before Lottie comes." Eddie looked around the room. "I think I got a lot of the cobwebs yesterday, although it was dark and I probably missed some."

I kept shaking my head. "I find it hard to believe she said she'd come over," I mumbled.

"She did. I'm telling you, she did."

"I'm tired. Didn't get much sleep. I'm going back to bed."

"Fine. I'll keep cleaning up. I want Lottie to see the potential of this place and give us suggestions."

"Whatever."

"And we should have something to eat, not just a drink."

"You said you just asked her to come over for a drink—not dinner!"

"She's not coming for dinner. She's coming at seven, but we still should have a little something to eat. What do you have here to drink?"

"Beer."

"That's it?"

"That's it."

"Don't you think you should get wine?" Eddie asked.

"Isn't it enough that everything's getting all cleaned and spruced up and she's coming over here to talk about something that I think might be a really stupid idea, to say nothing of the fact that she's probably still pissed off but was too nice to tell you she wouldn't come? I've got plenty of beer—can't we just leave it at that?"

"Fine," Eddie said, as he held up his hands. "Fine."

I went to my bedroom and shut the door. Luckily, I was able to sleep for over an hour because Eddie wasn't as noisy when he was cleaning as when he was sleeping. And I felt better with more sleep, and especially after I'd showered. I have to say it was weird seeing Eddie's stuff in the bathroom. I hadn't shared a bathroom with guys since I worked on a fishing boat in Alaska when I was in college, and that was over five decades ago. But at least there wasn't toothpaste squished on the sink and wet towels on the floor; Eddie had hung his up very neatly. So when I got up I told him I'd get some cheese and crackers at Thriftway. But my first stop would be the pharmacy. Earplugs were a priority after that terrible snoring last night.

I headed north on Wax Orchard Road; I prefer it to Vashon Highway because it passes the goats at the farm where they rent them out to be lawn mowers and brush cutters. It's a concept I quite like because you don't have to put gas in them. They are all different sizes and colors: white, brown, tan, black, some with different colored and shaped patches. Quite a few have nice little beards. And the horns—the big curved things that bend back and taper to a point can be very impressive, or some have thinner horns that seem to go straight up from their heads and only slightly angle out, and some don't have any. Maybe those are the females but I'm not sure about that. But I especially like their ears. A lot of them are small and pointy, but the long floppy ones are the ones I like best—I used to slow down and park on the side of the road to watch them, but I haven't done it much since Bess died.

My phone rang just as I was passing the goats and I pulled over to answer. Maybe Eddie thought of something else for me to pick up. But it wasn't Eddie. It was Martha Jane Morrison who lived below us on Baker's Beach.

"Oh George. I'm glad I got you ..." Martha Jane seemed to be in tears and could hardly get words out. "George, I just ..." Her voice broke. "I–I ..."

"Are you all right? Do you need help?" I tried to sound calm, but my heart sped up and my palms began to tingle which is what always happens when I'm very nervous. I had trouble comprehending at first. She's a strong, resilient person—warm, charming and seemingly unflappable. Bess knew her much better than I did, but I always felt like I knew her well because Bess talked about her all the time. Martha Jane was someone people came to for help, not the other way around. She was a person who never seemed needy and I was struggling to get my head around how shaken she obviously was.

"No, I mean yes ... I mean I'm all right, but—" Then she stopped talking, all I heard was sniffling. She tried to say something, but I couldn't understand her, and then nothing. "Would you like me to come over?" I didn't know what else to say.

"Oh yes, could you please ..." she was choking with little sobs, "there's a dead body..."

"A person?"

"Yes ..." she gasped.

"A human being?" I asked again, because Martha Jane loved all creatures with extraordinary reverence and passion. She didn't see humans as superior to other sentient beings and I could see her overcome by grief if an animal she was especially fond of had died. Maybe had died suddenly in some shocking way. But then it registered that she sounded frightened. And that was really unusual because she'd seen most everything (she's ninety-four) and was wise and philosophical about whatever life would dish out. Martha Jane had been one of Bess's dearest friends for years. I once said to Bess I thought she was probably the mother she always wanted, but Bess said Martha Jane was like Cinderella's fairy Godmother. So I said Bibbidi-Bobbidi-Boo, and then we started calling her that. Later it got shortened to Boo. We didn't say this to Martha Jane's face, of course. Although I don't think she would have minded. It was just the private pet name Bess and I had for her and almost every morning until the day Bess died she would say, "I'm going to have tea with Boo," and then she'd walk down the hill to Baker's Beach.

"Martha Jane, I just need to turn the car around. I'll be right there."

"It's on the beach ..." her voice caught and then I heard her trying to get her breath and she said, "I called the sheriff, but he's not here and ..."

"Don't worry. I'm coming." I turned around in Al and Bonnie Paugh's drive and headed south. Al is a retired veterinarian and I realized if it had been an animal, Martha Jane would have called him. (Now that I think about it, Al is someone I could ask about female goats and horns.) Al had rented a house on Baker's Beach next to Martha Jane's a few years ago after his wife left him (now he's married to Bonnie) and he and Martha

Jane became very close. Baker's Beach is a small community, a lot like Spring Beach and I figured Martha Jane's neighbors must not be home and I was the next person who lived close by.

She was sitting on the top step of her porch, bundled up in a blue puffy coat. Her hair, which she usually fastened away from her face, was spread around in a wispy white cloud like a dandelion gone to seed. Martha Jane's face has always reminded me of a pale pumpkin, a nice association because pumpkins make me think of pumpkin pie and Halloween, which are both things I like. Her wide-set blue eyes—which, although a little faded, still have the sparkle of her spirit, but now were swollen and red-rimmed from weeping. Martha Jane was hunkered down with her arms tight around her chest holding her cat underneath her coat, all except for its head which poked out of the top near her collar. At the end of the road right before the beach, about fifty feet down from her house, I saw an aid car and the sheriff's car.

"Oh, George ..." She shook her head, squeezing her eyes shut.

I climbed up the steps to the porch, crouched down beside her and took her hands in mine. They were cold, and fragile like little bird bones. "Let's go inside."

"I thought I should stay here in case the sheriff needed to talk to me again."

"He'll come to the door if he does."

She nodded and held her cat against her with one hand, and took my hand with the other as I helped her up. At ninety-four Martha Jane gets around pretty well, although her gait is slow and she walks gingerly, always looking down, conscious of where she steps to avoid falling. She has arthritis and Bess told me that for years Martha Jane never complained about it, but after she turned ninety she told Bess that when people ask "How are you?" she'd decided to tell them the truth. "I'm not going to automatically say 'I'm fine' like I've done for years. If my hip is hurting or some other part—I'll mention it. Just a fact, like a weather report and then we'll talk about other things." She told Bess she didn't want to dwell on it, she just reported it so they'd know how she really was. "And after I give the little report, if they say they're sorry to hear that, I find that I rather like it."

Martha Jane's house, like a lot of beach houses, has a damp seawater smell along with a hint of cedar and mildew. A few years ago she took up painting, so sometimes it also smells like oil paint, linseed oil and turpentine. She paints in the middle of the living room where the light is best and as we walked through to the kitchen, on the easel there was a painting of white and gray sea gulls sitting on driftwood. On the top of the easel Martha Jane had permanently fastened a sign:

USE THE TALENT YOU POSSESS BECAUSE THE WOODS WOULD BE SILENT IF NO BIRDS SANG BUT THE BEST.

In the kitchen she let the cat down and it scampered to the table and jumped up and sat next to the window. The little table was covered with a blue and white checked table cloth and in the center there was a small copper pot filled with dried flowers. I knew why Bess liked it here. The room itself was a cheery yellow with bright white woodwork trimming the baseboards and the frame of the wide window that looked out over Baker's Beach

"You should get down, Maria," Martha Jane said, without much conviction, and I wondered if telling the cat to get off the table was for my benefit because it ignored her and sat there staring out the window. Martha Jane had been a kindergarten teacher and the cat was named for Maria Montessori.

I helped her with her coat. I could tell her shoulders were stiff because she had trouble pulling her arms through the sleeves and it took a while to get it off.

"Thank you, George." She seemed calmer, although her eyes were still wet with tears. "I'll hang this up and then I'll make tea."

"I'll do it." I took her coat and pulled out a chair. "You sit down and I'll get the tea." She didn't argue and sat slowly, holding on to the table as she eased herself onto the chair. As soon as she was sitting, the cat scooted to her lap and settled there.

I hung the coat on a peg by the back door and then went to the shelf next to the stove which held various cups and mugs. None of them matched and most had slogans on them and I saw one that Bess had given her and reached for it. ALL YOU REALLY NEED ARE BOOKS AND CATS. It had been for a fund raiser for our local animal shelter. The one next to it said, IT'S NOT HOW OLD YOU ARE—BUT HOW YOU ARE OLD. I picked that one for Martha Jane. "Milk? Sugar?"

"Just plain. The box is on the counter and the water should still be hot."

The tea was the same kind Bess liked, Celestial Seasons Orange Spice, and after filling the mugs I brought them and sat across from her.

"Thank you." She put both hands around the mug warming them. The backs of her hands were covered with age spots like light brown raisins had been sprinkled across them. She looked out the window. "They must still be there. They haven't come up yet. The sheriff and the two medics. It's ... oh dear, I shouldn't call it an it. *He...* it was a he ... he was around the point in front of Walter and Maggie Hathaway's house." Martha Jane lifted the mug with both hands, bent her head down and took a sip.

"You found it, I mean him—"

"Yes. It was a him, I found him and then I called the sheriff and I would have called Howie and Mark, next door, but they're out of town and JoAnne McKee is on her lecture tour for psychiatrists for her sequel to her book *The Hoax of Penis Envy*, and she won't be back for another three weeks. And Walter and Maggie are traveling somewhere, but I forgot where. And Albert and Bonnie Paugh are visiting her son in Oregon. I'm just so glad I reached you, George."

"I am too."

"I don't mind being alone. I'm very good at it, as a matter of fact and Maria is the best company, but this really threw me."

"Understandably."

"I had left my rain parka on the porch and this morning when I looked out it was gone. I was sure it had blown off somewhere in the storm. I know I forget things, I have trouble remembering sometimes what I've done with something. But I was quite sure this wasn't the case and I went out to look for it. Even though there was no wind, I had to go slowly. Of course, that's how I have to do everything. But driftwood was scattered everywhere and I took two canes for extra balance. George, it's amazing all the stuff that ends up on the beach after a storm. There's water related things that you'd expect like buoys, ropes, beach umbrellas and chairs, and pieces of docks. But also things that probably come from boats—dishes, cups, plates and utensils and clothing and shoes. Well, as I headed along the cove, I saw what looked like a pile of clothes. It was in front of Walter Hathaway's house and it took me quite a while to make my way over there, but as I got closer I thought I saw my parka. I thought it had gotten tangled up in the pile of clothes, but ..." Martha Jane stopped talking and stared out the window.

"But it wasn't." I said, quietly.

"No. It wasn't." She looked at me and shook her head. "It wasn't. I went right up to it and—" Martha Jane put her elbow on the table held her head in her hand. She closed her eyes and took a breath before she could continue. "I could see that his hair had been white, he couldn't have been young, and his skin was the most garish color or colors I had ever seen, it's hard to describe them ... but his eyes were the most horrible. Like a dead fish staring. Oh, it was—grotesque."

We sipped our tea and neither of us spoke. But then we thought we heard voices and we both leaned toward the window and peered out. The sheriff was coming up from the beach; he walked pretty quickly to the road. There were two medics behind him carrying a stretcher and on it there was a black disaster body bag, all zipped up. We were glued to the window, not moving until the stretcher was loaded into the aid car, the doors shut, and the aid car and the sheriff drove away.

Finally, I asked, "I guess it wasn't anyone you recognized?"

"No, although his color and his bloated face ... I mean everything was so awful I'm not sure I could have recognized anyone I knew in that state." She took a last gulp, draining the cup.

"More tea?"

"Yes, thank you, George."

I took her cup, and waited by the stove for the water to heat up again.

"I can use the same tea bag."

"Okay."

"I can always get quite a few cups from one of those bags." She looked out the window again. "I can hardly believe this happened. The whole thing seems surreal."

"I'm sure it does."

"But George, I would like to know—know who he was."

"I suppose the sheriff will check some sort of list of missing persons and the *Beachcomber* might report it when they find out."

"I hope it's not anyone I know. What an awful thing, just washing up on the beach like some piece of rubbish. I don't know why it is, but death always seems to be a shock. No matter how many of my friends die, and most of them are gone except for my younger friends. It's a good idea to have younger friends."

I just nodded.

"What was I talking about? You know like a lot of old people I talk to myself. And I'm also trying to talk faster so I don't lose my train of thought and forget what I'm saying. But it doesn't always work, like now."

"About having younger friends?"

"Oh yes, and death. Thank you. Well, it's always a shock and I'm very familiar with it. Besides my friends, and of course my parents, I've lost both my siblings and all my uncles, aunts and all but one cousin, but she's pretty out of it. And I've outlived my husband, but death is still something I can't quite comprehend. One minute they're here and then they're not."

I brought the tea and sat down again.

She took a sip and looked out the window. "I've thought about it a lot and the only thing I've been able to figure out is that in order to keep living we have to deny all the dangers around us. I mean if we thought about them, we'd just stay in bed all day, or crawl under the bed. All the natural disasters, and then diseases, and accidents … something to end it all is always there just around the corner. And we have to try to deny the inevitable loss of loved ones because the loss is so devastating."

I didn't say anything. This whole thing was getting to me.

"So we get really good at blocking it all out, so when death comes it's a shock. Even when someone is sick and we know it's coming, it's still a shock. And then a lot of people say someone passed and not that they died. I know it's a way to think the body died, and the essence of the person passed from the body and went somewhere. But to me, it can be a way to avoid the fact that we die. So we can believe in some way we'll go on forever somewhere and that helps us face the fact that everyone dies. Sometimes I think we do that to soften loss and then also so we won't be afraid of all the things that can do us in, so we can keep going."

I wanted to tell her that without Bess I didn't think I could keep going, or didn't see the point in it. But I couldn't. The image of that disaster body bag loaded into the aid car was stuck in my head and I didn't want to talk about any of it. I scooted my chair back. "Well, I probably should get going. I was on my way to the pharmacy and Thriftway when you called." I stood up and put on my coat. "Is there anything I can pick up for you?"

"Actually, Maria needs some cat food. Do you think you could pick some up? But, I don't want to impose, you may not want to drive back here—you've been so good to be here with me this awful morning."

"Sure. I'd be happy to, what kind does she eat?"

"I appreciate that. She eats canned food, it's grain free and it's called—," she was quiet for a minute, then she said, "George, would it be okay if I went with you? I'd like to get out of the house and with the shock and all ... I guess I'm a little too discombobulated to drive myself. I still drive you know, but just on the island and never at night."

"Of course, it's more than okay." I got her coat for her and helped her on with it.

Martha Jane was one of a number of people in their

nineties on the island who were still driving. Vashon Island doesn't have any traffic lights, just a few blinking lights at intersections for an island about the size of Manhattan. And the only traffic, which wasn't much at all, was when the ferries from Seattle and Tacoma got in and the commuters headed home.

In the car I helped her with the seatbelt and then we headed out Baker's Beach Road.

"I appreciate this, George. I just didn't feel quite up to it. But I'm still quite a good driver if I do say so myself."

"I'm sure you are. Do you still drive on your missions to protect the deer during hunting season?"

"You know I think it's an outrage. They allow hunting for two weeks at the end of October, and it's mating season and the bucks are leaping around looking for the girls and even if it wasn't mating season two weeks is too much. One day is too much! I've tried calling our state representative—I forgot his name …" Martha Jane paused, touching her forehead, "Where was I going with this?"

"About the hunting."

"Right. Well, I've tried everything. So, as you know I've just had to take it into my own hands. Although I don't follow them and honk at them anymore, but since they mostly hunt in Island Center Forest, I stake out the parking lot and when I see some, I get out of the car and have a little talk with them. I usually ask if they have enough to eat, is that why they are hunting. And when they tell me they have enough to eat, I ask them why is it fun to kill a living, breathing creature? They usually ignore me, but I hope I've given them something to think about."

"That would be good. Especially if it took some of the fun out of it. If that's why they do it."

"I can't think of why else, if they don't need food." Martha Jane folded her hands on her lap. "Do you need anything at Thriftway? I hope you're not stopping just for me."

"No, I was going anyway. And even if I wasn't, I'd be happy to take you. Someone's coming over tonight and I guess I should have something to eat. I think I'll get Triscuits. Very few people know this but Triscuits were invented in the early 1900's and they are a classic cracker. You just can't beat a Triscuit. If you have to serve something, you can't go wrong with a classic cracker like a Triscuit."

"I like Triscuits very much. I didn't know that they are older than I am—not much is. It's weird being the same age as old people." she laughed. "So you're entertaining tonight?"

"I don't know if that's what you'd call it. It's all Eddie's idea. Eddie Mahoney. He's staying at my place now." Then I explained about Eddie's divorce and how he had no place to go and how he came up with this business idea so he could live at my house. "He acts very serious about the Airbnb thing, but I'm very skeptical. Lottie next door has one and she's coming over to tell us about it."

"That's very nice of her. Not everyone would want the competition."

"Oh, I don't think the Airbnb will really happen. I'm just going along with Eddie, since he's not in a very good place."

"He's getting a divorce, isn't that right?"

"He said it finally went through. His wife, Marlene—or now ex-wife, was friends with Bess and told her that Eddie was the youngest of four kids, he had three older sisters and they doted on him. And their mother thought he hung the moon. So he always thinks things will work out, but Marlene says that's because his family always bailed him out. All during their marriage he'd insist on doing various home repairs, things he'd do to save money—confident he could do anything—but it would end up a mess and then she'd have to get someone in to fix it. The worst was when he tried to make their living room and kitchen all one room and started bashing out a wall. The house almost collapsed."

"Well, you never know, maybe this time his idea might turn out."

"I'm not convinced. I'm just letting him stay with me until he figures out where he's going to go. He snores something terrible. I can hear it right through the wall and I was planning on getting some earplugs, so I'll need to stop at the pharmacy, too. Hope that's okay."

"That's perfectly fine. I'll just wait in the car. It's better than sitting at home wondering about the dead guy."

I nodded. "I was thinking I might stop at Granny's, too. To look at shirts. I'm a little behind on laundry." (Most of my clothes were in a pile on my closet floor).

"I'm happy to be out and about. I'm at a place in my life where errands count as going out."

"You're sure you want to go to Granny's? I can take you home after you get the cat food, and go back later myself."

"Oh, I love Granny's Attic. Those thriftway stores—" she paused, looking puzzled for a minute, "that's not what I mean, not Thriftway, the grocery store. I mean *thrift* stores. I have a friend who says that if you can't think of a word, just say 'I forgot the English word for that' and then people will think you're bilingual and not losing your marbles. But I got the word, didn't I? It was thrift."

"You nailed it, Martha Jane."

She grinned. "Thrift. Thrift stores. They are just the best for clothes and all kinds of things. I'd love to go to Granny's with you."

"Good. Maybe you can help me find something."

At Thriftway Martha Jane bought a special organic canned food for Maria, called Lotus Just Juicy Pork Stew Grain-Free, and I got the Triscuits. After that we stopped at the pharmacy where I picked up the ear-plugs and then we headed to Granny's.

As I helped her out of the truck she said, "Bess would be happy you're doing this, George."

"Going to Granny's?"

"Having people over."

"I talk to her, you know."

"I understand that." Martha Jane took my arm as we slowly walked across the parking lot.

"I haven't been in Granny's in a long time," I said, as we got to the front door.

"They always have new things."

"New old things, I guess. Sometimes dead people's clothes." I opened the door for her and looked around. "I keep thinking about the guy on the beach."

"I do too. But this should help us get our mind off

of him. Follow me. I used to volunteer here with Bess before my arthritis made me too slow, but I still know where everything is."

It's kind of amazing what cool stuff they have at Granny's. Bess was always commenting on the range and quality of what they had. But one time she donated an angel food cake pan with a bunch of other kitchen things that she didn't use much. It was after she'd read the book where the Japanese lady tells you to get rid of your stuff if it doesn't make you happy. About a week after she donated the pan, Maggie Hathaway, who lives at the north end of Baker's Beach with her husband Walter, was having her seventieth birthday and said her favorite cake was angel food. Bess went to Granny's and her pan was still there. She was happy there hadn't been a big demand for a pan like that.

We went to the area where they had men's clothes and began leafing through the racks. Clothes generally just get me confused and I pulled out the first one that looked like my size, a brown canvas work shirt. It looked in pretty good shape, but Martha Jane shook her head and grabbed a red one from the middle of the rack.

"See if this fits." She held it up to me.

"Oh, I'm not sure …" It was a western shirt, bright red with white trim on the collar, the cuffs, the front pockets, and a line across the shoulders on the back.

"And just look at these." Martha Jane pointed to the front of the shirt where instead of buttons, it had shiny white snaps. "Aren't these snappy?" She laughed. "I know, don't mind me, it's a little corny. I couldn't help it. Now just try it on, George, before you say anything."

"Should I go back to the dressing room?"

"Oh, I don't think you need to do that. Just slip off your shirt here and put this on right here."

I felt stupid taking off my shirt and standing there in the middle of Granny's in my tee shirt which was pretty ratty and had a little rip near the neck, but at least I wasn't standing there in my underpants. I handed my shirt to Martha Jane and I slipped on the red shirt quickly to cover up my ripped tee shirt. Martha Jane stepped close to me, reached up to my chest and began to snap the snaps. Her gnarled hands don't work all that well, but she insisted and was very determined to do it. It took a while, but I didn't take over the snapping—even though I thought about it. It seemed important to her to do it and I didn't want to make her feel bad or inadequate by moving her hands away and doing it myself.

"How does it feel?"

"Fits okay, I guess." I moved my arms around like a windmill and it didn't pull or anything. It seemed to be the right size.

"It looks very good. I think you should get it."

"Maybe it's too flashy." I looked at the price tag. Four dollars.

Martha Jane looked at the tag, too. "It's in good shape. It's a cheerful shirt and you can't go wrong at that price."

I was of a mind to just leave, run out of there and forget the whole thing. I'm not the cowboy type. I don't know what type I am, but Roy Rogers never appealed to me. I preferred Zorro. He had that nice cape and everything. Cool hat, too. But Martha Jane had been so kind, trying to help me and all, that I went to the checkout and bought the shirt.

When I dropped her off at her house, I asked if she thought she'd be okay. I didn't feel right about leaving her if she was still upset.

"I do feel better, thank you. And I plan to call the sheriff tomorrow to see if they've learned anything about who it is. I can let you know if I find anything out."

"I'd like that, thanks. And we might be able to get it out of our minds when we know more." I helped Martha Jane down from the truck and walked her up to the porch.

She opened the door, then turned back and gave me a hug. She held me close for a long time in her blue puffy coat with her arms tight around my chest. "I miss having tea with Bess in the morning. You should come down and have tea with me, George."

"I haven't been avoiding you personally. I just haven't wanted to do anything with anybody."

"I know about grief, believe me. It's the price … grief is the price we pay for love, but you should come down for some tea."

There was a lump in my throat, so I just nodded as I walked back to the truck. It had been a long time since I'd had a hug.

LOTTIE

I NSTEAD OF GOING STRAIGHT HOME WITH THE TRISCUITS, I went out of my way and drove to Lisabuela Park. It's a nice little shoreline park on the west side of the island, about five and a half acres looking over Colvos Passage. To the east of the park there's a wooded ravine and hillside, and in front of that a small parking area that overlooks the grassy play area, picnic tables and a hand carry boat launch. The park has an odd name, and when Bess and I first moved here we learned some of the island's history. The park had been the site of a post office and the guy who became the postmaster in 1892 named the post office for his daughters. Their names were Eliza and Beulah and he combined the names to be Lisabeula. (Bess always wondered why it wasn't named Lizabeula with a "z" if one of the girls was named Eliza.) And there were several versions of the history and it was never quite clear if the girls were the postmaster's daughters or some-body else's. But the name of the post office became the name of the park and Bess thought it was good that the guy named it for the girls and not himself. Over the years, the land had a lot of different uses and at one point a guy built a fishing resort there, the Lisabeula Resort, but it wasn't very successful. He was probably a lot like Eddie.

As I drove down the winding road to the park, the

Beatles song about the long, winding road played in my head. Especially the part "many times I've been alone and many times I've cried." I really hate that—when a song gets stuck in your brain and it keeps going over and over and you can't get rid of it. So I started humming "oblah di oblah da" and that helped to change the track in my head. At the end of the road I was glad to find the parking lot empty. I walked across the grass to a picnic table and sat there looking across Colvos Passage to the dark green hills of the peninsula. I could have been on the bank of a wide river, but the salt water tang of the air is unmistakably the sea. Puget Sound, which is now mostly called the Salish Sea, is the water that surrounds the island, but it belongs to the Pacific Ocean and when we have storms like we did last night it is a powerful reminder. I was tempted to go back to the car and get the Triscuits and eat a few. I didn't think it would hurt anything, who would know when I brought out the box that a few were missing? But I probably couldn't stop at a few, so I decided against it. Bess would say that showed self-discipline and maturity. Anticipating consequences and acting accordingly. But it's not always that easy. How could I have anticipated her leaving me without the slightest warning and shattering my life?

The sun was bright and there was a soft breeze coming from the south. I come here sometimes to talk to Bess, not that I don't talk to her everywhere. But it's quiet here and there are never many people so I can more easily hear what she would say. I like to watch the seals poke their heads up, and sometimes sea lions get close to the beach with their big round bodies. They make me think of her. Not that she'd appreciate that. (When I told her that the weight she put on over the years just made more of her to love, she scoffed and I don't think she believed me—but I meant it.) Even though the sun was out, it was chilly. I watched a seal pop up and look around with its big dark eyes. It was a gray harbor seal and its round little head looked silver in the sunlight. Bess had gray hair that looked silvery.

Bess. I miss you so much.

I know honey.

I saw Boo. She misses you, too. She said grief's the price we pay for love. If that's right, then I'll never quit paying it. And I don't want to because I can't be done with you.

You won't be. It will just soften to make room.

Boo found a dead guy on the beach. It scared me.

Don't be scared. You're not that guy.

How do you know?

Trust me.

You can't trust anyone not to leave.

My hands covered my face. I couldn't hear her. Only the cry of a seagull and that awful sound that it made ... or was that me?

George. I know it's hard to stop tears ... it's like trying to stop rain ... but ...

You'll say something about a rainbow next ...

You should go back home now, George.

I looked out at the water and the seal was gone, but I saw the round back of a big sea lion as it breached and dove down into the water. I was sure it was Bess. It happens all the time when I talk with her when I'm outside. Sometimes it's a bird or a squirrel. It makes me wonder if I'm nuts.

At home, about a half-hour before Lottie was supposed to come, I got in the shower and got dressed. I put on my new shirt. Eddie was sweeping again, but there wasn't as much dust as before. Just some leaves that we'd tracked in. I opened the Triscuits and put the box on the coffee table in front of the couch.

Eddie stopped sweeping. "I think you should put those on a plate."

"Why bother getting a plate dirty?"

"It's nicer than just plopping the box down." He put the broom away and went to the shelves next to the stove and took down a dinner plate. He rinsed and dried it and then handed it to me. "Here, put them on this."

I stared at the plate.

"What's wrong?"

"This is the first time I've used a plate since Bess died."

"What do you eat on?"

"Take-away cartons."

"You need to use your dishes, George. Why have them, if all they do is just gather dust?"

Dust—dust to ... I put the plate on the coffee table

and turned away and stared out the window. Dust to dust … ashes to ashes … I'll never get over how some little thing can just knock you over into a big puddle of grief. A wave—out of nowhere. It would have been dirt to dirt if that terramation method had been used for Bess, like one of her friends suggested, and she'd be turned into the dirt under a garden in the yard. And what if you stepped in the garden and got the dirt on your shoe? I squeezed my eyes shut and tried the kind of breathing that's supposed to relax you, although I never can remember if you inhale through your nose and exhale through your mouth, or vice-versa. And what is that dust to dust business, anyway? Wasn't it supposed to mean your body was made of elements of the earth? Like you're made of dust and return to ashes after you die. But I don't think people are made of dust. Mostly water, I think. The idea that Bess was mostly water and not dust made me feel better. I love water. I love living near Baker's Beach on the beautiful Salish Sea, the rightful name from the Indians of the Pacific Northwest and not the name of some random British guy who was one of those Brits who claimed they dis-covered it—when all those tribes had been living around the coast for thousands of years. I put the Triscuits on the plate and then saw Eddie reach for a couple of small plates, the ones Bess always used for salad. He rinsed the dust off and dried them. "Why do you need those little plates? This one is good enough for the Triscuits."

Eddie took two little cartons from the refrigerator. "I didn't think the crackers would be enough. So I picked up a few things from the Thriftway deli." He put some cheese and chicken drumsticks on the plates. "I'll put these back in the refrigerator until she comes."

"Chicken? What if Lottie's a vegetarian?"

"So, she'll just eat the cheese and crackers."

"Or one of those other veggie things, where they don't eat dairy?"

"Vegan. Then she'll just have a drink. It's no big deal."

I picked up the cartons and dropped them in the garbage. "Bess said everyone knows it's from Thriftway when you serve food from the deli and act like you made it. She said it was tacky."

Eddie crossed his arms over his chest. "I don't mean to be blunt. But you gotta stop worrying about what Bess would think. You need to think about our business and moving ahead."

"I just don't see why you got food. We just asked Lottie for a drink."

"To be a good host. Practicing for our Airbnb."

Eddie was getting on my nerves. I left and went to my bedroom and closed the door. I was starting to feel invaded by Eddie. He was getting too pushy. I caught a glimpse of myself in the mirror and I thought I looked ridiculous in the cowboy shirt. What was I doing? I should have been more emphatic. Just told him he could stay at my place as long as he needed to and left it at that. Not get sucked into this business thing. He could have stayed as long as he needed to because I do feel bad for him that Marlene divorced him, it could even be worse than if she'd died. At least when someone dies you don't feel they've had it with you. Not that you don't have regrets. I know I do. A huge one. What should I do Bess?

Keep going. One foot in front of the other.

That dead guy on the beach. It scares me that they won't find out who he was. No family to know he was gone or miss him. Like there was no point to his life. That he didn't really matter to anyone.

You matter, George.

Not anymore. Bess—I just …

"George," Eddie pounded on the door. "I see Lottie coming up the path. Better come out, now."

I opened the bedroom door.

"Come on now." Eddie grabbed my arm. "It's so nice of her to come to tell us about having an Airbnb. We both should greet her at the door."

"I haven't agreed to this yet," I muttered, and pulled my arm away.

"I know that," Eddie said patiently. "We're still just getting information."

I followed Eddie and we waited by the door. "I still can't believe Lottie said she'd come."

"I told you I'd pave the way. I said you felt terrible about getting stoned on the church field trip."

"Did she laugh? Bess always said when people laugh you know they're over it."

"She didn't laugh."

"This was a bad idea, Eddie."

"If she was still mad, she wouldn't come. Just remember what I told you to say to her."

I had thoughts of running downstairs and out the basement door. Maybe I could go down the hill to

Baker's Beach and see how Boo was doing. Eddie could make up some story about why I couldn't be there. He was good at making stuff up—thinking on his feet. But then there was a knock on the door and it was too late.

"Lottie!" Eddie opened the door and held out his arms for a hug.

"Hi Eddie." Lottie patted Eddie's back as they hugged, then stepped away and looked at me. "Hi, George."

I was frozen for a minute. I swallowed and then finally got the words out. "You look—you look very pretty, Lottie."

"Oh give it up, George. Just get me a drink," she said, as Eddie helped her off with her coat.

"A beer okay?" I headed to the refrigerator.

Lottie stood by the couch in front of the coffee table. "You don't have any wine?"

"I told you, we should have gotten wine." Eddie whispered to me, and then turned to Lottie. "Sorry about that."

"Beer's fine. Whatever." She sat on the couch and Eddie sat across from her.

I got the beer from the refrigerator and started to open it. Eddie motioned to me, then he held his right hand over his left and moving it in an arc, trying to tell me something—but I didn't get it.

"What?"

"Pour it in a glass, George." Then he stood up. "Excuse me, I'll give him a hand."

He went to the kitchen to get the cheese and the chicken drumsticks while I poured the beer in a glass for Lottie. I didn't see the point in dirtying up another glass, so I just took a can for myself. I went to Lottie and handed her the glass. I had to get it over with, so I just blurted it out. "Lottie, I feel really bad about what happened on the church field trip."

Lottie motioned for me to sit down. "I still can't believe you ate the whole package," she said, as she took a Triscuit.

"I was hungry. I did feel terrible. Kind of woozy."

"I would think. It's not the same stuff we smoked in the seventies." She chewed the Triscuit and then reached for another one.

"True. I behaved badly and I'm really sorry."

"So ..." Lottie nodded and gave me a funny smile, "would you recommend those brownies?"

"In moderation." I looked at Lottie and she laughed, so I laughed, too. I glanced up at Eddie in the kitchen and he gave me a thumbs up. "And I also want to say I appreciate your keeping Max in at night."

"That wasn't for you. I was worried about the coyotes." Lottie took another Triscuit. She was about to put it in her mouth, but she stopped and stared at me, leaning toward me with her eyes squinting like she was trying hard to see something. She looked at me, just staring and staring for the longest time. Then she said, "George ... What's that you're wearing?"

"A shirt. I got a new shirt. It's a cowboy style."

"I can see that."

"I don't think I'm really the cowboy type. I did like Zorro, though—he had a cool hat."

"Where'd you get it?"

"At Granny's."

"Ha! I thought so. That's my husband's shirt! I finally

got around to getting rid of his clothes." She took a bite of the Triscuit.

"Oh, well. Do you want it back?" I would have been happy to give it back to her. I thought it looked dumb on me.

"No, I don't want it back. It just gave me a start, that's all. What if I showed up in Bess's clothes? How would you feel?"

I took a swig of my beer. "I haven't gotten rid of them yet. Maybe I should avoid Granny's."

"Go to the Goodwill in Seattle. Unless you don't mind running into someone at Thriftway wearing her favorite outfit."

"I can change my shirt." I started to get up.

Lottie motioned for me to sit down. "Oh, forget it, George." She took another sip of her beer as Eddie came in with the plate of cheese and the chicken. He put them on the coffee table and then went to the desk and got a piece of paper and a pen and sat down next to me, across from Lottie.

"So Lottie," Eddie held the pen in the air, ready to write, "how long have you had your Airbnb?"

"A year. And it was the smartest thing I ever did. Bill didn't have that much life insurance and with the property taxes going up, the income has been great. And I meet interesting people from all over."

"The room in George's basement would be our Airbnb. It's got a separate entrance and its own bathroom."

Lottie nodded and reached for a chicken drumstick. "That's a good selling point."

"The toilet's backed up," I reminded Eddie. "I think it's the septic and I'm waiting for the septic guy to come."

"Good luck with that," Lottie took a bite of the chicken. "You can be waiting for Godot."

"His name is Scottie, not Godot," I said and saw Lottie roll her eyes as she chomped on the chicken.

"Godot was—oh never mind." She held the bone of the drumstick up and looked at her hands. "How 'bout a napkin?"

"Would a paper towel be okay?" I asked, as I went to the kitchen.

"Sure. Whatever." Lottie said, holding up the chicken bone.

"I use them for napkins, wiping up stuff—they're all purpose." I tore off a few sheets of the paper towel and brought it to Lottie.

"I could use one, too." Eddie said, so I gave him a sheet and took one for myself and put it on my lap.

"I hope I don't have to wait too long for the septic guy to come. He said I'm first on the list. He's new to the island."

"What did you say his name was?" Eddie finished his chicken and put the bone on the paper towel.

I went over to the table by the wall where my computer is and found the paper where I'd written down his name. "It's Scottie's Septic Magic."

"So his name is Scottie, something?" Eddie asked.

"Right. Scottie McDonald."

"He should get a better name," Eddie said, "septic and magic don't really go together."

Eddie had a point, I thought. "Sort of like peanut butter and tuna fish."

"Exactly," Eddie nodded. "It should be jelly."

"As soon as it's fixed the bathroom should be good to go," I said to Lottie.

"Good for people to go! Ha-ha!" Eddie cracked up. It was a dumb joke, but it got me laughing, maybe it was nerves, just a huge relief of how tense I was with Lottie there and I tried to stop but I couldn't control it very well and that made Eddie laugh harder.

Lottie glared at us. "This is ridiculous. I'm wasting my time." She started to get up.

Eddie put his hand on her shoulder. "Don't go!" He sounded kind of desperate. "We want to learn from you."

"Oh, all right," Lottie said and she sat back down. "We were talking about bathrooms."

"Yes. Bathrooms," Eddie said, and wrote that down.

"Right. Bathrooms." I tried to sound serious, not wanting to lose it again.

Lottie sat back and crossed her legs. "Bathrooms are very important. Everything has to be spotless, of course, and people like nice towels and special little soaps. At Costco I get a lot of toothbrushes."

"Don't they bring their own?" That sounded weird to me and I looked at Eddie, wondering if he thought this was weird, too. But he was smiling at Lottie and nodding his head.

"In case they forget." Lottie said. "It's a nice thoughtful thing to have for them. And the bed is very important. I got a new mattress and lovely bedding. My beach house can sleep four with the sofa bed. The more you can accommodate the better."

"Can't the extra ones bring sleeping bags?" I asked.

Lottie leaned forward. "Look, it's very competitive. A lot of people on the island have Airbnb's and if you say extra guests have to bring sleeping bags, it's not going to cut it."

"That's very good to know." Eddie said, "A very good point."

"I put fresh flowers in the beach house and I have a small refrigerator stocked with fruit and cheese. I set out wine glasses and a bottle of red and put white wine in the refrigerator."

"Huh?" I couldn't hide my surprise. "I didn't think this was supposed to be a restaurant."

"She's not saying that, George." Eddie looked up from his notes. "Just to have these nice extra things."

"Local wine is especially good, " Lottie explained. "People like local touches. And you'll see on the Airbnb website that some hosts offer experiences."

"Experiences?" This whole thing was sounding sillier and sillier. "That sounds kind of kinky."

Lottie glared at me. "Boating, kayaking, guided tours, cooking classes—"

"Like George's famous recipe," Eddie laughed. "Step one: go to the Thriftway deli. Step two: pick out the food. Step three: open the carton and dinner is served!"

"Don't forget napkins," I said.

"Are you guys serious, or what?"

"We are! We are!" Eddie waved his notes around.

"I haven't bought into this deal yet," I said.

"Well if you do, you need to think of a charming name."

"For my basement?"

"I call my beach house Happy Isle Hideaway."

Eddie wrote it down. "People would find that appealing."

"You could give the septic guy a few pointers," I said.

Lottie ignored me. "But the most important thing is getting good reviews. If you get a bad review your business is toast. They have six things they rate you on. The first one is accuracy."

"What's that supposed to mean?" I asked.

"If you list your place as a charming cabin in a serene meadow and it's really a dumpy shed behind somebody's old barn. It's not accurate."

"Like those bald guys who are seventy," Eddie chimed in, "and they put a photo on Silver Singles when they were forty and had hair."

"Exactly. And communication is another thing they rate. You should respond right away to emails and phone calls and be very friendly." Then Lottie ticked off the rest of the things on her fingers. "There's cleanliness, location, and value—meaning, if it's a good deal for the money."

"I still can't believe anyone would pay to sleep in my basement."

Eddie put down the pen. "If we fix it up, like she says."

"I read a review that said the host played classical guitar and the people raved about it. Little extra things can help a lot." Lottie looked at her watch. "Well, I have to get home to Max," she said, as she stood up. "Thanks for the beer and good luck."

Eddie and I followed her to the door. "Thanks for coming, Lottie." I said and held the door open. "And again, I'm sorry about—"

"Life's short, George. I'm over it."

"Thanks for the help, Lottie!" Eddie called to her as she headed up the path. He closed the door behind her and turned to me. "She's right! Life's short—that's why we've got to move ahead with our business."

"This whole thing—all this fussing over people sounds like a huge hassle. Besides, I don't know what the septic guy is going to find."

"Try to keep an open mind, George. Remember how Lottie said it was the smartest thing she's ever done?"

"I'm not Lottie." There was a desperate cheeriness to him so I went to him and put my hand on his shoulder. "Listen, Eddie. If you need a place to stay, you can count on being in my spare room. Just stay as long as you want."

"I appreciated staying here last night," Eddie said, looking down, then went to the coffee table and carried the beer cans and the empty plates to the kitchen. Finally, he said, "I guess thinking ahead has never been my strong suit." He got a paper towel and went back to the coffee table and began wiping it. "You know I really didn't mind it that much—living in the attic with Marlene in the rest of the house. Peaches would come up to see me." Then he smiled with a false little swagger, "I'm kind of a live-in-the moment kind of guy."

"Look, it's no trouble to have you. It doesn't have to be this business deal."

"Thanks. And that means a lot." Eddie went to the refrigerator and got another beer, then went to the couch and sat down. I got one, too, and sat across from him. I could understand that a guy had his pride, but maybe he would be able to admit what was going on—that he needed some help.

"Like I said, I appreciate being able to stay here. I really do, but I'm very serious about the business. It's a great opportunity. Just tell me something, George—what do you look forward to?"

I took a swig of the beer. "Not much. The way I see it we're swirling around the drain." That actually made me think of that alkaline hydro-something method, or whatever it was to get rid of the dead body. The one where they turn people into liquid and wash them down the drain.

"George, what do you look forward to?" Eddie asked again, like I hadn't heard him.

"I heard you—and I don't know what I look forward to. I don't think about the future, all the funerals we go to are about the past. We've been going to so many lately, you even started rating them."

"The one last week was a four star. Great food. Great music ..."

"The cookies were kind of stale, I thought."

"Maybe a little, but overall it was pretty good, the slide show went nicely with the music. But listen, we need to look forward to more than going to good funerals." Eddie finished his beer and took the can to the kitchen. "Guess I'll go unload all the rest of the stuff from my truck now."

"I'll give you a hand."

"No need. You're doing enough for me already, George."

I didn't say anything. I went out and we unhooked the bungee cords on either side of the big tarp covering his stuff and together lifted it off his truck.

UNCORKED BY MARTHA JANE

I HAD A TERRIBLE SLEEP AGAIN. NOT BECAUSE OF EDDIE'S snoring—thankfully, the earplugs I'd gotten at the pharmacy were taking care of that problem. It wasn't that, it was the dead guy. Crazy, creepy dreams woke me up and when I would finally get back to sleep, there'd be another awful one. So disturbing that I'd find myself leaning forward, propping myself up on my elbows, my eyes darting around the dark room trying to orient myself. In my dream the dead guy was a guest at an Airbnb. His body lay decomposing in my basement, and I couldn't get rid of it. Every time I tried to pick it up, pieces of greenish flesh started floating away. It was horrible. In another one, my basement turned into a funeral parlor and the dead guy lay in a casket and there was a very good funeral with "Amazing Grace" playing on an organ, and tasty food, which included Triscuits, put out for a reception after the service. But no one came. And the body lay there for months, rotting away little by little until it completely disappeared and there was no trace that it had ever been there at all.

I don't know when I got back to sleep, but Eddie had coffee made which was nice to have when I finally got up. Around nine he left for the post office to put in a change of address card, to list my house as his new address. I thought he might as well, because there was no telling how long he'd be here. After I fed the chickens, I gave Martha Jane a call. I was trying not to refer to her as Boo in my mind, because I was afraid I'd forget and blurt it out sometime and it would be awkward. I don't much trust my memory, but Bess never had that problem.

"I hope I'm not calling too early—"

"Good morning, George. No problem, I've been up for a while. I needed to fill the birdfeeder. I've been waiting for the goldfinches to arrive, and the first one of the season arrived this morning!"

"Bess didn't think it was really spring until they showed up."

"We agreed on that, like most things. I know some people think it's the crocuses that are the sign, but I've known crocuses to get snowed on. The goldfinches are the most reliable indicator."

"I was wondering if—um, if I could take you up on your offer—if that's okay."

"Why yes, of course. But just remind me, what offer was that, dear?"

"To come down and have tea."

"Wonderful. Come on down whenever you'd like. I'm not going anywhere."

"I don't suppose you've heard anything about the dead guy?"

"No, but I plan on calling the sheriff's office. I would think they'd tell me since I was the one who found him. I'll call in a few minutes. Maybe I'll know something by the time you get here. When did you say you're coming?"

"I guess I didn't, maybe in a couple of hours—would that be okay?"

"Of course, I'll have our tea ready."

I had just thrown on the jeans from my closet floor when I went to feed the chickens and I thought I should shower and put in some laundry so I could wear fresh clothes to visit Boo, I mean Martha Jane. As I gathered my dirty laundry and took it to the washing machine I thought about how Bess went to see her almost every morning. It was a morning ritual for her like the way some people do exercises or meditate or pray.

The shower is another place where I talk to Bess, something about the warm water all around makes me feel more calm and less overwhelmed because the only thing I have to do is wash and I can manage that. It doesn't take much effort, unlike feeding the chickens. As I shampooed my hair (or what's left of it) I admitted to her how stuck I still feel … my whole life has been gridlock the last two years and it's never let up … totally stuck, not going anywhere. But I'm just not sure this Airbnb is the thing to unstuck me. Besides, Eddie gets excited about all his ideas, but he never thinks anything through. He's never realistic. I just don't know about it.

> *You've got to cut him some slack. You should listen to this Hebrew proverb I heard—Hebrew is big here. It says, "You will never have a friend if you must have*

one without faults." You know how to do this. You never made a big deal about my faults, you always cut me slack. Just give Eddie a chance. Give it a try.

It just seems like a hassle.

You haven't tried much, George.

I tried the Church of the Holy Tree.

You never should have eaten all those brownies.

It never would have happened if you were here.

So it's my fault you got stoned on the church field trip because I died ...

I know you're laughing but ... I didn't mean that. You always helped me. You would have helped with the nightmares about the dead guy. I wonder what you'd say about where dead people go? If there's a soul or something like that. What's it like there?

No rules or anything. you're just supposed to try to put God first, the other person second and yourself third.

Didn't we hear some minister say that?

Maybe.

What's he like? I mean she?

Who?

God. You used to say it was a she.

It doesn't matter. Depends on who you talk to. I've heard God's a tree … someone else said a dog … and there's this lady who thinks it's Elvis. And the people who wear the colanders on their heads …

The what?

The bowls with holes where you drain pasta. They call themselves the Pastafarians. I'm not exactly sure about them. They might think God is pasta. Anything goes really, and no one tries to shove their idea down anyone else's throat, so it works okay. But we're talking about you here, George. You've got to get a grip.

I miss you. I've been lonely, Bess.

I know.

I've been so lonely I stayed on the phone with this solicitor lady. She was trying to sell me time shares in a resort. I let her talk and talk, but when I didn't give her my credit card she got mad at me. It was very unpleasant.

It's been two years, George. You could talk with people if you do Eddie's idea. The other things you've tried didn't work, so why not do this with Eddie?

I suppose you mean the yoga class.

I don't remember the details. Just that it didn't work.

I went once. I was the only guy in the class.

What happened?

They showed us how to do downward dog like this. (I bent over to wash my feet.) Well, there's no polite way to say it.

Oh no. You didn't.

A blast like the foghorn on the Tacoma Narrows Bridge. The women tried not to laugh. But there was a little giggle, then another one, then the whole place cracked up … I never went back.

I can understand that.

Are you laughing?

Only with you. But you've got to try again.

I'm done with yoga.

Not yoga. Something new. Eddie's right. People need something to look forward to. It's like hope. Hope is an end in itself. Try to remember that.

But Bess …

Go ahead now.

I wanted more of her, but as I turned off the water and got out of the shower, she had faded.

It was close to eleven by the time I got my clothes out of the dryer, got dressed and headed down to Baker's Beach. I hoped Martha Jane really meant it was okay for me to come now, so close to lunch. I worried that maybe she'd feel like she had to feed me. Like offer a nice egg salad or a tuna salad or something, with a dill pickle and some chips. I put my hands in my pockets and looked at the little green buds on the trees. The sun was warm on my face. She was right that it looked like spring was here to stay. It was probably in the high sixties and the bright blue sky had big fluffy clouds like you'd color in kindergarten. There were times when a day this beautiful made me feel terrible. When it was dark and rainy it matched how I felt, but the sun with everything sparkling and bright would make me feel really crappy. I'd think, how could I feel so crappy when it was so beautiful? I should feel cheerful! And when I couldn't get cheerful that would make me feel even more terrible.

Martha Jane waved from the front window when she saw me coming up the steps and went to open the door for me. "So nice to see you, George. Come on in."

"Thanks," I said, and followed her into the kitchen.

"You look very spiffy this morning."

"I did some laundry. I think I smell better."

"My sense of smell isn't as good as it used to be, but you look wonderful. Now have a seat and I'll get our tea. Same kind as yesterday, okay?"

"Sure, thanks." While she made the tea, I looked around the kitchen and thought about how Bess had sat in this very seat, at this very table almost every morning for years. I wondered if my being there might make Martha Jane miss Bess more. Here I was showing up for tea the way Bess did, but I wasn't Bess. I could never take her place. No one could. Usually, I didn't think about the other people who missed Bess. But Bess and Martha Jane had been so close—Bess totally trusted her and I'm sure it was mutual. If Martha Jane had confided any secrets to Bess she'd certainly never said anything to me.

I glanced at Martha Jane pouring the hot water into the mugs. She wore navy sweatpants and a red sweatshirt with a strawberry on it that was from one of the island's Strawberry Festivals. Her soft penguin shape and wispy white hair made her seem completely safe and unthreatening. But I began to wonder how much Martha Jane knew about me. How much did she know about me and Bess? About our marriage? Some women tell each other everything. This made me feel weird and so uneasy that I thought maybe I should just say I forgot something and tell her I had to leave.

She brought the tea and sat across from me. She walked slowly and carefully, but it seemed easier for her to get herself in the chair than it was yesterday. Maybe the sunshine helped her arthritis. It didn't seem right to just get up and leave right then. Maybe after I finished the tea.

"So," she said, taking a piece of paper from her pants pocket. "I called the sheriff and he hadn't found out who the man was, but he told me how it works." She put on her glasses and read from the paper. "The body is taken to the King County Medical Examiner's office and they keep it for about twenty-one days while they check the missing person data base. They assign a case number and record where it was found, the gender, race, approximate age, height, and weight, and describe the clothes the body had on. And if the body didn't have any identification, like no wallet or something found on them that said who they were, then sometimes they make a sketch of the person's face and post it on their website with the details they had."

"But if the face is all messed up, how accurate would it be?" I couldn't help wondering.

"Oh, well, I never thought of that. Maybe they have special artists or people for that."

"Or a computer. On TV I've seen things like that."

"Could be."

"What happens if no one shows up to claim the guy?" I asked.

"Well, they can't keep that many unclaimed bodies around so they cremate them, but then they store the ashes in a secure location at the King County Medical Examiner's Office. And then if no one comes after two years, they bury the ashes in shared plots, but in individual containers. But they keep the records for each container, so they can be recovered if someone shows up to claim them."

"You mean if someone shows up to get the ashes."

She looked up from the paper. "I think that's what it meant."

I took a sip of my tea and looked out the window. It certainly was the calm after the storm. There was so little wind the leaves on the trees at the edge of the beach hardly vibrated and only the slightest waves touched the shore. But the big driftwood logs and other debris from the sea littering the beach were a reminder of the storm and the death it had brought to Baker's

Beach. "Martha Jane, do you remember that mother Orca whose calf died, and she swam around for a long time with her dead baby on her back?"

"It was heart breaking. What made you think of that?"

"Maybe the dead guy didn't have anybody. At least the calf had its mother for a little while. That whole thing made Bess so sad. She felt the same way you did. She said it broke her heart to see the mother not being able to let go."

"Bess was a sensitive person."

"She was." I had almost finished my tea and it seemed like a good time to head home.

But I didn't. There was something compelling about being with Martha Jane. Something magnetic and I wasn't able to pull myself away. I tried to get a grip, telling myself to go, but I sat staring in the mug at what was left of the tea. Across from me she was quietly sipping her tea; we were both quiet. And then, as if my voice was something I was not in charge of, I heard myself telling her, "I always thought someday Bess would leave me. I never really knew why she stayed with me."

Martha Jane patted my hand. "George, she was grateful to you and over the years she came to love you very much."

Hearing that really got me and I was afraid I'd lose it, weep into the dregs of my tea like some slobbery drunk crying in his beer. But at least I didn't have to explain. She probably knew all the details. "She confided in you a lot, I suppose."

"We shared quite a bit. And trusted each other. In a small place like the island, things get around. You have to be really careful who you confide in and Bess was one of the few I felt I could tell anything."

I had finished my tea and had been there a while so it wouldn't have been rude to leave—but I stayed. Because I understood then why Bess came here every morning. Getting a hit of kindness, and caring—and acceptance. You could get addicted to it. It uncorks your heart, and although I have always been a private person (except with Bess) where keeping things to myself has been the safest way for me to navigate an unpredictable world, I went on talking. Even talking about what I suspected wasn't news to Martha Jane.

"I guess you probably know that she had been kind of a wild child. Not by today's standards, of course. But she went for the bad boys. Like the guy who, you know …"

"From what I understand, she was under quite a bit of pressure at home and found it suffocating."

"I'd been in love with her since junior high, you know."

"Really? I didn't realize that."

"We were in the same homeroom. Beasley, Braxton— they organized them alphabetically so every morning from 8:00 to 8:30 I would be near her, sitting just a few feet away and it kept me going during the darkest days when things got so bad at home. It was all I could do to keep from staring at her, she was that beautiful. When everyone else was at that geeky, pimple-infested age, Bess was stunning. She looked like a young Grace Kelly."

"She was a beautiful woman, even as she got older," Martha Jane smiled.

"She always wanted to lose the weight. But I really didn't care. I think she knew that. I hope she did."

"Of course she did, George. You're not one to say anything you don't mean."

"I'm not a salesman type, that's for sure. In high school, the junior class had to sell raffle tickets to make money for some class event, I don't remember what it was now. But I was terrible at it, I didn't sell any—not a single ticket—so my mother felt sorry for me and bought them all. She'd just been diagnosed, but she still thought about me. And what she could do for me."

Martha Jane patted my hand again and I hadn't planned to get into it all, but then I did.

My brain was on the history channel and couldn't switch out of it. "It was my senior year and I was going to turn eighteen in July. I'd worked every summer at Boeing and would again before I started at UW in the fall. The lawyer said it might take a while to sell the house, but when it did and the hospital bills and outstanding debts were paid, whatever was left would go to me. It wasn't a huge fortune or anything like that, but I didn't see why I couldn't stay in the house until it sold. And when it sold, I could live in the dorm. The University of Washington wasn't that expensive back then. But Rev. Braxton, Bess's father, suggested I move in with their family. I know he felt sorry for me. Everyone did. Orphans have that effect on people. Although, I guess technically I wasn't an orphan. After my mother died, the lawyer found a cousin of hers, Dottie Fletcher. She and my mother exchanged Christmas cards every year, but that was about it. She lived in Pahrump, Nevada and she wanted no part of a teenage boy she'd never met, which was fine with me—the name of the town was weird. It sounded like someone gagging and I didn't think a town with a name like that would be a good place to live. Besides, I didn't want to leave Seattle. So when Rev. Braxton suggested I live with them, I jumped at it. I know a lot of guys my age would have pushed to stay in their own house, wanting the freedom. But I didn't think twice. Because of Bess." I closed my eyes, remembering what it had been like at night, that spring when I was seventeen. Sleeping in the room next to Bess's, longing for her so much it hurt. And then hearing her open the door, to sneak out at night.

"Martha Jane, you know how they say when you're drowning your whole life passes in front of you? But it's like I've been drowning for two years and my whole life with Bess is passing in front of me."

"It doesn't have to be one or the other. You can have all your memories of the past, but try to be in the present, too."

"That's what Bess says. I can hear her, you know. Do you think I'm crazy?"

"No. She's part of you, you know what she would say."

"Frankly, I don't really want to be in the present."

"I understand that. But that's where we are and we have to make something of it."

"Bess would say that."

"I'm sure she would."

"She would want me to have this business with Eddie. He wants me to have an Airbnb in my basement with him. She would want me to do it—but I don't know ..."

Martha Jane smiled. "I think you should, too."

"You do?"

"Yes. Absolutely."

It was Martha Jane's conviction that morning that made up my mind. That, and the idea that if I ended up a dead guy on the beach, at least Eddie would know I was gone and he would go claim me from the King County Medical Examiner's office.

PARTNERS

I ALWAYS WONDERED WHEN MY MOTHER WAS YOUNG IF SHE had gone for the bad boys the way Bess had. I'm sure my father fell in that category and I had his name, George Beasley, Jr., but as I got older the main effect he had on me was to inspire me to be as different from him as I possibly could. At some point I dropped "junior," although I don't remember when. A big handsome guy, my father wasn't what you'd call a mean drunk, he was just totally out of it a lot, completely pickled, so much so that he'd lurch in the house and pass out, especially after he lost money at Longacres Racetrack. His ship, or more accurately, his horse was always going to come in.

I think going to church helped my mother. It was a respectable escape, although I later wondered if she wasn't in love with Bess's father, Rev. Braxton. He was the one who encouraged her to attend Al-Anon which met at the church every week. I was ten when my father left us, so that had to be 1957. It was right after he got fired from Todd Shipyard for drinking on the job. When I was a sophomore in high school, Mom heard from his sister that he'd died. Supposedly, he wanted to come back to us when he got sober, but it never happened and he was hit by a car crossing a street in Reno.

After Bess and I had been married a long time and after her parents had died, I told her I thought my mother had probably been in love with her father. She wasn't surprised. "Most of the women in the congregation were," she'd said, and was quite matter-of-fact about it. And when I asked her if her mother minded, she said, "George, you know my mother was a church-mouse." She didn't say it in an angry way. Bess knew a lot about her mother's early life, mostly from her Aunt Nan, her mother's youngest sister, and I suppose it helped her to understand and eventually accept who her mother was. Although I don't know if her disappointment ever completely went away. I think it probably faded, as if the years sanded down the sharp edges of disappointment. And I'm sure resentment, too, that her anxious, timid mother, could hardly stand up for herself—let alone anyone else. Bess was as far from that as you could get. Her personality was more like her father's; she was passionate, charismatic and enthusiastic. She also looked like him, although her coloring was from her mother. She certainly got the best of both of them.

Bess's mother, Carol Hansen, was from eastern Washington; her family had a small wheat farm and she met Bess's father when he had to drop out of Whitman College during the depression and found work on their farm. She was the fourth of the six Hansen girls and when Bob Braxton showed up, not only did she fall in love—she practically worshipped him. Bess always thought something in her father needed that kind of totally devoted adoration.

In their wedding photos, her mother was very pretty, although when I knew her she seemed brittle and fragile looking. Rev. Braxton was strikingly handsome, with a full head of hair and a Kennedy-like smile—Carol would have done anything for her husband, and she did. As soon as they were married she started work as a packer at an apple farm which helped put him through college, and after his graduation when Bob went to the School of Theology and Ministry at Seattle University, she worked as a file clerk in a nursing home.

Bess's father became the minister of a community church near the University of Washington, where a lot of the congregation taught at the University. "I think it was a fork in the road," Bess told me. "Dad was earning a salary and she could have gone to college, it was certainly her turn after she'd put him through both college and graduate school. And I'm sure he would have been for it—but it never happened. I think the congregation intimidated her and made her feel inadequate and she was afraid of being a student where she'd be graded and judged. My mother chose the safe road where she wouldn't have to put herself out there—just stay in the background and not risk anything. It was always the way she operated in the world, avoiding anything that made her anxious or uncomfortable. As a consequence, she had a narrow life where almost any shred of self-esteem was totally tied to him."

I was thinking about my mother-in-law's cautious life and wondering if my reluctance to go into business with Eddie made me like her. But it seemed different to

me—I just didn't want a hassle, something else to deal
with. I suppose there was a possibility that Eddie's idea
could work, unlike so many of his flakey schemes—
although it seemed pretty remote to me, and I had my
doubts. But the main thing was, at the end of the day,
I decided I didn't want Bess to think I was a wimp like
her mother.

I was reading the *Beachcomber,* carefully looking through
the paper in case there was something about the dead
guy being found on the beach. I didn't see anything
about that, so I got myself a beer and waited for Eddie,
who was outside with the septic guy. When he came in
about fifteen minutes later, I told him.

"I guess it's okay," I said.

"What is?"

"The business. This Airbnb business."

"We'll do it together? Be partners?" He grinned,
rocking back and forth on his toes.

"I guess so."

"Awesome!" He jumped up and practically leapt
across the room and punched me in the arm, which I
didn't appreciate. I guess I didn't look as excited about it
as he had hoped because after a minute he said, "You're
not going to change your mind now, are you George?"

I had to think about that. I wanted to be honest
with him. "I told you, you can stay here as long as you
need to. And if the business turns out to be too much
of a hassle, we can just forget about it and hang out
and go fishing like a lot of retired guys."

"You just said you'd do it!" Eddie threw up his hands. "Besides, you let your boat go to hell after Bess died."

"Okay, okay—I said we could give it a try. But there's no way the Airbnb can open until the toilet's fixed."

"I know that. Jeez! You think I'd want guests to come here with a broken toilet?"

"I didn't say that."

"Okay, but look—we don't have to wait to get everything else ready." Eddie started pacing with arms behind his back and his hands locked together like the way Prince Charles walked. Then he stopped. "The guy's been here for two days, what's taking so long?"

"It's probably not that simple. I had the tank pumped a few months ago, and only the basement toilet is backing up."

"One of life's little mysteries, I guess." He went to the computer. "I'm going to check out some other Airbnb listings. Lottie's right—the one's with good names get attention. We have to decide on our name."

While Eddie was looking at the computer Scottie came up from the basement. Scottie McDonald was a stocky bald guy, with a broad face and droopy whiskers (I think it was supposed to be a mustache) that made me think of the walrus at the Pt. Defiance Zoo. He smelled pretty bad, but I didn't comment on that because after all he'd been digging in the dirt where a toilet pipe had broken. I just stepped back and put my hand up to my nose. He was wearing tan coveralls and had light blue foot covers over his boots. "I worked my magic! Finally found the problem!" He was carrying a clipboard and he tore off an invoice and handed it to me. "Tree roots had gone into the pipe so I replaced it and you're all set."

I braced myself and looked at the amount and tried not to gag. (Not at the bill, but the way he smelled.) I knew I had been lucky to even get someone without having to wait forever. Island time was a fact of life here, even under the best of circumstances; and after a big storm, anyone who can fix things is in demand— especially plumbers, which is basically what septic guys are. They can get away with fleecing you if they want. Scottie's bill was $459.72 and although it was an expense I was not thrilled about (to say the least!) I couldn't complain because it seemed to be in the ballpark of what it would cost. He also seemed like an okay guy (in spite of the weird name of his business, and the way he smelled, which of course went with the territory). Besides, being new to the island, I was sure he wanted to get off to a good start. "So everything else with the system is okay?"

"Just the one pipe."

Eddie looked up from the computer. "That's a relief."

As I went to get my checkbook, Eddie stared at Scottie. "You really look familiar. Not too many Scottish accents on the island. And your voice—"

"Septic Magic is just my day job. Maybe you heard me sing around town," he said, mentioning a couple of island restaurants that sometimes had musicians.

"That's it. I remember it now. You sang Scottish ballads."

Scottie must have taken that as a cue, because he put the clipboard on the floor, lifted his head, spread his arms wide and burst into song.

"Maxwellton braes are bonnie …
Where early fa's the dew … And 'twas there
that Annie Laurie … Gave me her
promise true … Gave me her promise true …"

I had finished writing out the check and stared. It was bizarre to see this stocky bald guy with his droopy mustache smelling like Pigpen emanating septic fumes singing at the top of his lungs in the middle of my living room. I didn't know what to say so when he stopped singing—covering my nose with one hand and extending my arm—I handed him the check.

"I appreciate your business. Call me anytime to work my magic." He picked up his clipboard and walked toward the door.

"Wait … wait!" Eddie ran over to him. He seemed oblivious to how bad the guy smelled.

"Forget something?" Scottie turned to Eddie.

"George and I are going to open an Airbnb—would you consider singing for the guests?"

I glared at Eddie. "I don't know about this."

"I'd love to!" Scottie grinned.

"What's it going to cost?" I barked. It was just like Eddie to jump into something without thinking it through, and this partnership was off to a lousy start if Eddie thought he could just do stuff without talking to me. I was pissed.

Scottie thought for a minute. "I'll tell you what. Since you're just starting out—I'll make a special deal. The first gig is free. After that $25 for an evening of beautiful ballads. Your guests will love these old favorites—'My

Love is Like a Red Red Rose'—and 'Black is the Color of my True Love's Hair'—I've got a ton of 'em!"

"I love it," Eddie said, "let's do this."

"For a little extra, say ten dollars, I can bring my bagpipe."

"Oh for God's sake," I hissed.

"Let's just start with the singing." Eddie said, ignoring me as he put out his hand and he and Scottie shook on it.

Scottie waved and went out the door singing. It must have been his outside voice—it was so loud I thought he could be heard by picnickers over at Pt. Defiance Park in Tacoma.

> *"AND FOR BONNIE ANNIE LAURIE ... I LAY ME DOON AND DEE ..."*

"Let's get one thing straight, Eddie. You can't go deciding stuff without asking me—or that's it!"

Eddie held his hands up, like he was surrendering. "Okay, okay—you're right. But I had to jump at that, seize the opportunity before the competition snapped him up."

"Competition!" I yelled. "You think all the Airbnb's on the island are lining up to book the singing septic guy?"

"You don't have to shout, George."

"Who's shouting? I'm just making a point, here."

"Look, you never know what's popular. They have bagpipes every year in the Strawberry Festival parade. People love them."

"I don't want a bagpipe in my house. I thought we were talking about singing."

"I was just making a point about Scottish music

being popular, that's all. And you never know, word travels fast here. Lottie said the Airbnb with the classical guitar had amazing reviews." Eddie hurried over to the computer and sat down. "The toilet's fixed, so there's no time to waste. We've got to get listed!"

"Well, don't decide any more stuff on your own."

"Not a chance. Now we've got to settle on a name. We'll decide it together."

I went to the kitchen and got a beer. I had half a mind to tell Eddie to forget the whole thing. I didn't have anything against Scottie McDonald but having the septic guy singing in my house wasn't what I thought I was getting into. I sat down in the plaid chair and drank my beer and picked at the hole where the stuffing was coming out.

Eddie looked up from the computer. "For the name, I'm thinking we should go with the Scottish theme. We need to brainstorm." He stood up and started pacing. "... Bonnie Bluebell Basement ... Highland House ... Scotch Broom ..."

"That's a weed."

"I'm just brainstorming ... Piper Place ... Lassie Lair ... Bonnie Wee Basement."

"Nook sounds nicer than basement. How 'bout 'Nice Nook'?"

Eddie perked up. "You're on to something with 'Nook.' How 'bout 'Bluebell Nook'?"

"We don't have any bluebells." I took a swig of my beer. "Besides, I let the garden go. It's a mess."

Eddie kept pacing, ignoring me. "Bluebells are Scottish. There's a song, *Bluebells of Scotland*. We can have Scottie open with that one. Or do you like Magic

Nook better? Or Magical Nook? Magical is a very popular concept."

"I don't think my basement is magical. And we
don't have any bluebells."

"So we'll plant some."

"And you'll weed and water them?" I just shook my
head. I could see why Eddie liked "magical." He thinks
things just magically happen.

Eddie went back to the computer and sat down.
"We're getting off track here. There's no time to waste.
We have to fill out the listing form, I'll go with Bluebell Nook," he paused and looked over at me, "unless
you have an objection."

"Whatever." (I felt like saying, I don't give a rat's
ass what you name it.) But I held back and went to
take my beer can to the back porch where we had the
recycle bin.

"If you're leaving, George, I'm just going to have to
make the decisions on this form myself."

"I was just going to the porch," I said, but instead
I got another beer and sat in the plaid chair because I
didn't want Eddie deciding everything.

"Okay. Number of bedrooms ... one." Eddie said,
as he typed.

"Right."

"Bathroom ... one." Eddie kept typing.

"Right."

"Accommodates ... two. Check-in time ..." He
looked over at me. "What should we say?"

"I don't know. What does Lottie say on hers?"

"I'll look." Eddie stopped typing and put in a search
for Lottie's listing. When he found it he told me her

check-in time was 3:00 pm, and check-out was noon. She offered free parking and she allowed smoking outside.

"Okay. So copy all that," I said.

"And for internet, you have to give them your password."

"I don't want to." I took a swig of my beer.

"Look, if we're going to do this, we have to do it right. We have to be competitive."

"Oh, what the hell. Whatever."

"What about pets?" Eddie looked over at me. "Shall we allow pets?"

"Bess is allergic to dogs. That's why we didn't have one."

I loved dogs. We had one when I was a kid, Rob. He was a mutt that had a lot of cocker spaniel in him. Rob was like a brother to me. Maybe better. A lot of guys I know fought with their brothers when they were kids but there was no rivalry between me and Rob. I could talk to him and I told him things I would never tell anyone. There was a horrible kid in my class, Russ McIntyre, who bullied everyone, and I was a favorite target. He called me Measley Beasley. I'll never forget the guy, even after all these years. I've read that bad memories get rooted in our brains and are very hard to dislodge. I think there's some truth to that. I remember McIntyre especially went after me in PE when we had to play dodge ball. It's hard for me to admit this because it doesn't sound that bad, but what a terrible game—kids trying to smash each other with a hard leather ball. What kind of sportsmanship can you learn from that? At our school they only allowed flag football, but they thought dodge ball was okay. They probably didn't count on someone as nasty as Russ McIntyre. I wasn't completely un-athletic (in high school I ran cross country) but I didn't have the kind of quick speed and aggression you need to play that stupid game. I found no pleasure in getting clobbered with a ball or trying to hit anyone else with it. I just tried to keep out of the way and duck. McIntyre had that hostile sixth sense that can intuit weakness and fear in a person. He'd seek me out and bellow, "Take that! Measly Beasley" and aim for my balls. I hated the guy and I told Rob about how much I hated him. I told him that I wished Russ McIntyre was dead. If I told that to a person, they'd think I was terrible for wishing someone dead. But not Rob. He loved me for who I was. When Rob died, I sometimes think it was harder for me than when my dad left. Rob was hit by a car and had to be put down, which I always thought was a weird way of saying that your dog was going to be killed by the vet. But his injuries were so awful, they just wanted to put him out of his misery. I understood that was the humane thing to do, but I was unspeakably lonely, and it took me a long time to really accept it. My dad left not long after that and Mom went back to work as a secretary at the Dobson Plumbing Company. She didn't want another dog because it would be alone all day when she was at work and I was at school. Rob was such a great dog. When I think about it, I still miss him.

"George, I understand that Bess was allergic but—"
"Okay, okay. They can have pets."

"How much should we put down for the cleaning fee and a security deposit?"

"In case they wreck the place!"

"It's just standard. I'll copy Lottie." Eddie typed some more. "Now, we have to list some of the special things we'll offer. I'm putting down live music at the cocktail hour provided by a renowned local ballad singer. And then we can offer bird walks and boating."

"What the hell are you talking about? *Bird walks?*"

Eddie got up and went to the window. "See that bird out there? That's a chickadee. We'll walk around the yard and point out the birds. I'll buy a bird book and we can look up the birds that come to the yard."

"I don't believe this. What about boating?"

Eddie walked back to the computer and sat down again. "We can take the guests out in your boat."

"It's a twelve-foot boat with a five-horse motor. I'd hardly call that boating. Besides, you already said it was a mess because you know very well, I haven't cleaned it out since that otter crapped in it."

"Okay, it would probably take too long to clean it and we want to open right away. How 'bout guided tours of the island. We can take them to the lighthouse at Pt. Robinson."

"They don't need us for that. This is ridiculous."

"Oh all right. I'll delete bird walks, boating and guided tours of the island. We'll just go with the ballad singer at cocktail hour. So, I'll put down your phone number and email for the reservations, and we're all set."

"Stop. Don't list it yet."

"Why not?"

"It's not ready! We have to clean up, make the bed, get towels and nice soap and the stuff Lottie said."

"Okay." He stood up and went to get his coat. "I'll get the ferry and go to Target and get those things and you clean the room."

"No."

"No?" Eddie stared at me.

"We're doing everything together or not at all. I'm not cleaning the sink and toilet while you go shopping!"

"Fine. It will delay the listing, but if that's what you want that's what we'll do."

MORNING TEA

I T WAS BECOMING A REGULAR THING, MY GOING DOWN TO Martha Jane's for tea most mornings. I didn't want to be a pest, but she reassured me that she liked my company and she always did seem happy to see me. I felt close to Bess when I was there, and Martha Jane and I would talk about her. Some people, like Eddie for instance, are uncomfortable when you mention a dead person. Maybe they don't like talking about something so sad and they try to change the subject. Or they don't know what to say. After my mother died, I remember how jarring it was. I felt so cut off from the world, it was just moving on as if nothing had happened, but my world had turned upside down, and I couldn't put the two things together. There were people who pitied me—I could feel it and I didn't want that. It made me feel weak, but by the same token I didn't want them to act like nothing had happened. Business as usual. I think it's a hard note for people to hit: to acknowledge your loss but at the same time not feel so sorry for you that you feel pitiful.

It was another beautiful spring morning with a vivid blue sky and fluffy white clouds that made me think of vanilla ice cream. The buds on the trees were getting bigger, no longer tiny soft green dots, but a green so fresh and bright the leaves almost looked chartreuse. The daffodils lining the path to Martha Jane's house were in full boom, a butter yellow that made me think of having toast (with jam—and not just butter) if Martha Jane offered me some, which she did as soon as I got there.

First, I slathered the toast with butter. It was wheat bread with different seeds in it, even a few tasty little nuts. I'm sure it was very healthy. I finished covering it with butter and then with peach jam which Martha Jane's neighbors Mark and Howie had given her. They made it themselves and put on their own label which they made on their computer. HOWIE AND MARK'S IMPEACH JAM. It was delicious.

"I haven't made any progress on finding out who the dead guy is," Martha Jane said, "but I did find an interesting article in the archives of the *Beachcomber*. It seems our fellow isn't the first one to wash up here."

"That's really sad." I put a little more jam on my toast. "Another person ending up like that."

"But surprisingly, it wasn't as sad as you might think. It was a woman who was just shy of her nine-tieth birthday and her eyesight was failing and she was increasingly experiencing dementia. And in a note to her daughter, she said she'd had enough and was ready to go. And she walked into Puget Sound from Titlow Park in Tacoma. The tides and the currents carried her body to Vashon, and her daughter said she couldn't help but find a bit of mystery, magic and even poetry in the way her mother's life ended. She had lived on

Vashon, her closest friends were from here and she loved the island. Her daughter said it was like karma."

"I don't think anyone would think the way our guy ended up was poetry."

"Maybe not, but we don't know about him yet. The way this woman was described in the paper, she seemed like a special person, with a great sense of adventure. She'd gone into the Peace Corps at sixty."

"Like Miss Lillian."

"Lillian who? Do I know her?"

"Jimmy Carter's mother. She went into the Peace Corps when she was 68 and she worked with people who had leprosy in India. Bess really admired her."

"Oh yes, I remember now. You know, I used to feel that older people who did great things like that put the rest of us to shame. Like the ones who go mountain climbing when I feel it's an achievement getting my leg through my underwear without losing my balance. But now I just admire them and try to appreciate that we're all made differently, and we don't need to feel diminished by these extraordinary people. To me it's like we all can't be Sonja Henie but that doesn't mean we can't have a lovely little skate around the pond. Or if we don't skate anymore, just enjoy looking at it."

"Sonja Henie? I take it she was a famous ice skater?"

"Before your time, George. She was Norwegian and she won all kinds of Olympic and World titles. More than anyone ever has, I think. I'm part Norwegian you know, on my mother's side, so I closely followed her career." Martha Jane sipped her tea. "What were we talking about before Miss Lillian and Sonja Henie?"

"The lady who walked out in the sound and her body washed up on the island."

"Oh, right. Well, I read that her daughter said her mother had lived on her own terms for a long time and she was completely at peace with her mother's decision."

"I envy that. That you could lose someone and be at peace. I guess it depends on the circumstances. I mean if your loved one was murdered, how could you be at peace?" I went to get more hot water for my tea.

"George, I think we should name the dead guy."

"Really?" I sat back down across from her. "Aren't we waiting to find out who it is?"

"It may take a long time, and it doesn't matter if it's nothing like his actual name. But after reading about the woman who washed ashore here—a real person whose daughter obviously loved her, I just think we should stop referring to him as the dead guy."

"Okay by me. Do you have any names in mind?"

"I do. I'd like to call him Woody—"

"That makes me think of Woody Woodpecker. Shouldn't we get something more respectful, if that's the idea?"

"Not the woodpecker. Woody for Woody Guthrie, the great folk singer and song writer. He wrote 'This Land is Your Land' and 'This Train is Bound for Glory' and 'So Long It's Been Good to Know Yuh.'"

"Perfect. Better than the woodpecker. Did you just think of that now?"

"I've been thinking about it ever since I read about the woman who washed up here."

"Names are hard—Eddie and I finally came up with one for our Airbnb. It's Bluebell Nook."

"Bluebell Nook—" She smiled. "That's charming, George. It's a lovely name."

"We don't have any bluebells, and my basement isn't really a nook. But we went with it anyway. Eddie put the listing on last week, but we haven't had any interest in it, which, to tell you the truth, is fine by me."

"Bess would approve of what you're doing—she'd be cheering you on."

"I know she would. The things that worry me wouldn't bother her if she was the one doing it. Like if terrible people came and wrecked your house, or you spent all this money on little soaps and fancy towels, and no one ever came and you felt like a fool. Bess had a sense of adventure. And she was very inventive—did she ever tell you about what happened with two of our chickens?"

"If she did, I forgot. I forget a lot of things, George. Not only what people tell me—but what I've told other people. That's why I always say, 'Now if I've told you this before—don't stop me' because what's the harm in telling it again?"

"None that I can see."

"Now what were we talking about?"

"Bess and the chickens."

"Oh, right. What about them?"

"It was one summer when we had a big hot spell. The temperature was close to 100 which, as you know, is very unusual here. Bess discovered two of the chickens had keeled over from the heat near the fence post. They lay motionless on their sides with their eyes like little beads of black glass and their legs stiff. She thought they'd probably died, but just in case she scooped them up, one under each arm, ran to the house and put them in the freezer."

"The freezer?" Martha Jane looked puzzled. "You mean the freezer for frozen food?"

"Right, on our refrigerator it's a separate compartment on the top. It's the only freezer we have. We never wanted one of those big stand-alone freezers because we lose power so often. And we'd be stuck with a whole freezer full of spoiled food. So Bess lay the chickens in the freezing compartment on top of some packages of spinach and lima beans. After about a half hour, Bess opened the freezer and the chickens were standing up, blinking at us and looking very perky. I'm not sure how it would have been if she'd kept them there much longer—I don't know how much air is in there or how much they need. But they were completely revived and good as new. Like I said, she was inventive. She was one to try things."

"I would think the chickens were grateful."

"Oh, yeah. I'm sure they were, being resurrected in the freezer. I wish people could be brought back that easily."

"We're not supposed to live forever, George. I think we have to try to live our best life with whatever we've been given and hope that when the time comes there just aren't too many regrets."

"If Bess had been at the end of a long life and things were going downhill and she felt like she was a burden—if she'd had enough—I can actually see her being brave enough to walk out into the sound like that lady did. She was one to take risks. And I'm almost the opposite." I put my cup down and looked at Martha

Jane. "The thing I've never understood—even though I know why in the beginning she chose a boring person like me—the thing I've never understood, is why she stuck around. But I know I said that before."

"She loved you."

I nodded and looked out the window at two seagulls hopping along the beach. "His name was Vince Kelly. I suppose you know that."

"George, it was a long time ago that Bess talked to me about it. I know some people my age are fed by their memories, which is fine. I do that too, but I also try to stay in the moment—be in the present. Be present. Another goldfinch came to the feeder this morning. Now that was a lovely moment."

The seagulls had taken off and were sailing over the water swooping around each other and I wondered if they were mating, or just pals hanging out. I turned back to Martha Jane. "He was the kind of bad boy she had a thing for—he looked like James Dean, not in *Giant* but in his first big movie, *Rebel Without a Cause*. Except he had black hair and black eyes. His mother was Italian and his father was Irish. Rev. Braxton didn't approve of him and her mother was clueless."

Martha Jane sighed. "Bess loved you, George. I'm not sure it does any good to revisit the past like this, but it's clear you need to talk about it."

"I've never talked about it to anybody before."

"Well, I can certainly confirm that Bess saw her mother as dutiful but ineffective. Someone who was very anxious and mostly seemed to care what others would think. In my experience people like that are so caught up in their own distress they can't see others.

They can't be there for them or tune into them in any consistent and genuine way."

"That's how it was, and Bess couldn't talk to either of them. Rev. Braxton was always out at church meetings, and when he was around, he was constantly on her case for something. Bess always felt they loved her for who they thought she ought to be, not for who she was. They wanted her to be perfect. And I would have done anything for her. That's why I covered for her when she was with Vince. We'd leave together to say we were going to the library. I had my mother's car and I'd drive to the library parking lot where Vince would be waiting for her. His car was a turquoise and white 1957 Chevrolet Bel Air with loud mufflers and my mother's car, which had become mine after she died, was a gray Ford. The cars said it all."

"I remember Bess said she felt bad about using you like that. She said you weren't a goodie-goodie, you were just good."

"I was a very willing participant. I would have done anything to make her happy and she appreciated me covering for her—and that meant a lot. Vince Kelly was a total jerk, but he was an exciting jerk to her and I'm sure on some level it was a way to stick it to her parents. He was four years older than Bess, he'd graduated in '61. He'd been a football star in high school, a great running back, but when he went to the U he couldn't handle not being the star. There were guys from California who were much better—and he was a big drinker. He would have been cut from the team if they'd found out, but he ended up flunking out and went on to work at a car wash and sell weed. Not exactly a parent's dream."

"No, I would think not. But she didn't end up with him, she ended up with you."

"She did. By default." Martha Jane has a way of getting me to talk. She doesn't pry, so I don't know how she does it. I guess it's just something about her, so it's possible I might have stayed longer and gone into all of it—but my phone rang. I pulled it out of my pocket and saw that it was Eddie. I thought about ignoring it, but then I worried that maybe something was wrong. He hardly ever calls me. I apologized to Martha Jane and told her I thought I'd better answer.

"George, you gotta get home right away!" Eddie was practically shouting.

"What's wrong?"

"Nothing! We have a booking! The email just came in and the people apologized for it being last minute, but they want to know if they can come today and they asked us to call them. So you better come right home and call them."

"Why can't you call them?"

"I had to get Peaches. I have to take her to the vet because Marlene—oh, never mind, I'm on my way there now—it's a long story. Remember how Lottie said communication is very important and you get rated on being prompt answering emails and phone calls? So you have to call them right away."

"Why can't you call them while you're waiting at vet?"

"Because they'd hear all these dogs barking and whining and stuff and it's not professional. For God's sake, George, are we partners or not? Do you want to put the kibosh on our business before it even starts?"

"Okay, okay. I'll be home in five minutes and I'll call them."

"Good. The number and everything is in their email. This is it, George—*Showtime!*"

I explained to Martha Jane why I had to leave, and she grinned and got up and slowly walked me to the door. "I'm so glad you've decided to do this with Eddie, George. It's going to expand your life. Meeting new people, having a new focus—it can be very stimulating. And when guests feel taken care of, they're very appreciative. And the knowledge that you've provided them with a lovely experience will be very gratifying."

A RESERVATION

I KNOW I SHOULD HAVE BEEN ENCOURAGED BY MARTHA Jane's optimism and Eddie's excitement, but it had the opposite effect on me. I don't like talking to strangers. Eddie's good at it. He can talk to anybody and when I agreed to be partners with him, I naturally assumed he'd do most of the talking. It takes me a long time to feel comfortable, and I worried that when I called these people I would say something stupid and they'd change their mind about Bluebell Nook. Then they'd try to find another Airbnb and if everything else on Vashon was booked and they were determined to experience an island—sailing on the ferry on the Salish Sea and all—they'd try some other island like Orcas or Lopez.

As I walked up the hill from Baker's Beach, instead of feeling relaxed and enjoying looking at the trees the way I had on my way down to Martha Jane's, I continued to feel tense. It was nothing new. It had always been hard for me to talk to people. In fact, Bess was the first person in my life that I ever found easy to talk to. I've thought about it a lot and I'm sure part of it was because she was completely unattainable. With Vince Kelly being the guy she was crazy about, well, it just made her safe to talk to—also, she was incredibly kind to me. She was kind to everyone, but she was a witness to what it had been like for me when my mother got sick. They didn't have hospice back then, but Rev. Braxton and the Women's Auxiliary Guild at church made sure someone was always with Mom at the hospital. One time I got there after cross country practice and both Rev. Braxton and Bess were there. Bess's dad was by Mom's bed, holding her hand and he said, "Don't worry about your boy, Alice. We'll take care of him, won't we Bess." And she said, "We'll be there for him, Mrs. Beasley."

And Bess and I, in our goofy teenage way, were there for each other. She trusted me with her secret relationship with Vince Kelly. And I trusted her with everything.

When I got home, I saw the email that Eddie had printed out and left on the desk. I put on my glasses and picked it up.

From: bco'grady
To: Bluebell Nook
Re: reservation

We realize this is last minute, but we would like to stay at your Airbnb tonight, and are hoping to take the 3:30 ferry from Fauntleroy. Please call us as soon as possible so we can make other arrangements in case your room isn't available. Our number is 555-363-2127

Bob and Cathy O'Grady

On top of the email was a sticky note from Eddie. It looked like he'd scribbled it in a hurry, but I could still read it.

> It's an Irish name—that's close to Scottish! They'll love our singer—I'll track down Scottie and pick up food for them as soon as I'm done with Peaches!

I checked my phone to make sure I had enough battery. It wouldn't be cool to have my phone die in the middle of the call. Not professional, Eddie would say. I looked at the phone number. I thought area code 555 was one of the new ones on the east side of Lake Washington where the cities were growing so fast. Microsoft was there. What if Bob O'Grady was some super rich techie guy? Was that sexist, assuming it was the guy? Maybe Cathy was the Microsoft superstar, or they both were, and on a whim, they decided to come to Vashon and everything on the island was booked except Bluebell Nook. But wouldn't the O'Grady's have their own fancy plane, probably a seaplane and they could fly anywhere, and since they were so rich they probably had an amazing second home, or third or fourth home and if they wanted to get away from the city they would take their plane to that home that looked like some magnificent home you'd see in the movies with a tennis court and an indoor and an out-door pool and the outdoor pool had a beautiful little waterfall cascading into the pool and they could swim naked whenever they wanted because their magnifi-cent home was so secluded.

George ...

I could hear Bess as I stared at my phone thinking about the rich and famous life of Bob and Cathy O'Grady.

> *Just do it, honey. You can do it.*

I don't know about this, Bess.

> *Just be yourself.*

Myself? I look in the mirror and I don't look like anyone I know anymore. Just some old man. And around young people I'm invisible.

> *That's your superpower, George.*

I wish I did have some power. When guys age, their testosterone dwindles and they just turn into little old men, little old dears.

> *The world could use more dearness and less testosterone.*

But I'm still uneasy around new people. It's stupid. I should have gotten over it by now, I'm in my seventies!

> *George, we take our insecurities to the grave, believe me, I know about this. So you just do things in spite of them. Go ahead now, honey.*

I knew she was right. You can't wait for the insecurity to go away, you just have to go ahead in spite of it. That was exactly what Bess would say, the kind of thing she always said. I could sense her with me so I closed my eyes, took a deep breath, looked at my phone, and breathing her in, I called the O'Grady's.

A woman answered. Her voice sounded clipped and efficient.

"This is George Beasley calling from Bluebell Nook on Vashon Island, I'm calling for Bob or Cathy O'Grady..."

"This is Cathy—we know it's late notice, but Bob and I would like to book a room tonight if you have a vacancy."

"We do have a vacancy this evening and we'd ... we'd ...

> *Love to ... George, tell her "love to."*

"love to have you stay with us."

"Great. How close are you to the ferry?"

"About fifteen minutes."

"Is there parking?'

"Oh yes, parking is not a problem."

"It's possible we'll probably want to stay an extra day, would the room be available the next night?"

"An extra day would be fine."

"Good."

> *Tell her you're looking forward to meeting them, George.*

"We're looking forward to meeting you," I said, "we'll see you and Bob tonight."

I hung up and told Bess that I guessed it wasn't so bad. But she didn't seem to be there anymore, and just then Eddie came in and I knew I wouldn't be able to find her voice with all Eddie's chatter. He bounced into the kitchen with a grocery bag, and while he put away the wine and the food he'd gotten, he began grilling me about the phone call.

"Did you get the O'Grady's? What did they say?" Eddie stared at me like a puppy waiting for a treat.

"I did. I talked to the woman, Cathy. She wanted to know how long it took to get here from the ferry, and then she asked if they could stay an extra day."

"I hope you said yes!"

"Of course I did—you wanted me to pretend we were booked or something?"

"No, no … forget it. I just want to know everything you said." Eddie folded the grocery bag. It was one of the cloth ones Bess had gotten from the World Wildlife Foundation with animals and their logo on it and he put it in a cupboard under the sink. I have to say Eddie had been good at making the kitchen more tidy—and the whole house, too. "I think we're in good shape," Eddie said, looking around, "although maybe I should dust a little."

"I don't see any dust."

"You can't see up close without your glasses." Eddie got a rag from the broom closet and started dusting. "So, you were friendly to the woman?"

I got some coffee and sat down in the plaid chair. "I told them I was looking forward to meeting them."

"Excellent," Eddie said, as he flicked the rag over the desk.

I thought about the cloth grocery bag with the WWF logo and some of the other things Bess had from organizations we contributed to. We didn't have all that much of what you'd call discretionary income, but we gave what we could, and Bess liked having the things they'd sometimes send you when you made a contribution. She had a lot of tee shirts from things like Planned Parenthood and Amnesty International, and non-profits on the island, too. I started picking at the stuffing coming out of the hole in the arm of the chair. "Eddie, what if the guy shows up in one of those red hats?"

"The red hats are for women. It's some kind of group for old women. Marlene was in it. She told me it came from a poem where the lady said when she's an old woman she wants to spit and wear purple, or something like that." Eddie moved over to the table by the couch and started dusting the lamp.

"Not that. You know, the political one—we don't see many of those on the island."

"Oh. That red hat." Eddie stopped dusting and looked over at me.

"I don't want a guy in that hat staying in my basement."

"I understand that, George. But you really can't ask people about their politics before you book them."

I poked the stuffing back in the hole. "Why not?"

"It would be like that bakery that wouldn't make the wedding cake for the gay couple."

"That was bad. But I don't think it's exactly the same."

"I suppose it's complicated, but you get the point."

"Oh, whatever." I didn't want to argue about it. "Did you get Scottie?"

"I called him when I was at the vet. He has a septic

job on the north end of the island and he'll be here after he gets cleaned up."

"Well, I would hope so."

"He said he would. There's no reason to think he wouldn't."

"I meant getting cleaned up after working on a septic."

"That's ridiculous. Of course he would." Eddie went back to dusting and I left to take a nap. Calling the O'Grady's and then having it dawn on me that I had no idea who they were and these total strangers would be staying in my house and I'd have to give them food and be nice to them, no matter who they were, well, it just got me tired. As soon as I closed my eyes Bess was there and I told her that I didn't know what I'd gotten myself into.

Don't worry about it. I know you're anxious around people you don't know, but you know I've always said you just do things in spite of it.

You said people take their insecurities to the grave, but you never seemed to have any. You always had confidence.

Not really.

It seemed that way to me.

Fear doesn't go away. Worries don't go away. You just keep going.

You had such great energy and stamina and warmth. I know people wondered what you were doing with boring George.

Well, anyone dumb enough to think that didn't know you like I do.

But I wondered, too. Why you stayed? What you saw in me?

Do I have to spell it out?

Try me.

You never once criticized me or told me what to do. Never blinked when I had a big piece of pie, or two ... or piled on the ice cream.

I remember your joy when you discovered mochi ice cream at Thriftway.

One time you told me that bodies are just the houses we live in and as the years go by, the foundation wobbles, the porch sags, the paint cracks, but the person you love is in there as good as ever.

I said that?

Maybe I heard it on TV. But that's how you treated me. Like a was a treasure inside this old house.

Get some sleep now, George.

THE O'GRADY'S

THE ARRIVAL OF THE O'GRADY'S FELT LIKE A MILESTONE. I was doing something that to me seemed significant in that it didn't involve Bess; it was something she would never be a part of no matter how real she seemed in our conversations. It was different somehow than the previous pathetic attempts I'd made to jettison myself out of my desolation: my aborted attempt at yoga, the likes of which could have been a memorable skit on the old Sid Caesar show if they'd allowed fart jokes back then, and the Church of the Holy Tree fiasco with my getting stoned on the brownies. Those little dalliances in trying to carve out a new life for myself as a widower involved no obligation to anyone and I could bail whenever I wanted to, which I did after both brief ridiculous episodes. No, this was different. Bluebell Nook had a website and was officially affiliated with Airbnb, the worldwide vacation rental online marketplace. No fly-by-night crackpot scheme, it had been around since it was founded in 2008, and Eddie had even sent in the paperwork to the state for a business license.

The recognition that this was a milestone did not inspire confidence. When I had been trying to get up the nerve to call the O'Grady's, I worried I would be so awkward they would decide Bluebell Nook wasn't for them—now part of me wished the O'Grady's would cancel. Maybe their fancy dishwasher broke and flooded their fabulous kitchen, or Cathy's Mercedes got rear-ended, or Bob fell off his special power bike and broke his toe when he was riding home from Microsoft. Or maybe they would change their mind and not show up without bothering to tell us. Because that's the type of rude and inconsiderate people they were: very entitled with all their wealth, with never a thought of how they affected others. Fine by me. Although it would be a disappointment for Eddie— he was so pumped about this whole thing. But Eddie was resilient in his own weird way because he wasn't afraid of failure, which was hard for me to understand because he'd had quite a few schemes that fizzled and not just the lawn chair balloon festival. One time he started an oyster farm with a guy who had a waterfront cabin near Reddings Beach and the oysters died after a week. I think he lost a few thousand dollars on that. He also started a fishing school to teach kids to fish. He advertised in the *Beachcomber* and had a ton of tee shirts made with MAHONEY FISHING SCHOOL printed on them and he paid a designer to create a logo with a kid and fish bunched around the letter M. The design lady charged Eddie something exorbitant—I'm pretty sure it cost more than all the shirts. And no one signed up for the fishing school. Not a single kid. I always wondered what he did with all those shirts; he bought several hundred of them because there was a deal that each one cost a little less if you bought a big quantity. That was back when he had his boat before Marlene made him sell it because trying to keep it running was throwing money down the toilet.

I had an hour before the O'Grady's were supposed to arrive, so I put on the Mariners game. Bess and I only had the one TV and kept it in our bedroom. We both liked watching sports and we watched movies and the PBS Newshour, but that was about it. Oh, we did watch Charlie Rose regularly before he got in trouble. We missed him, and Garrison Keillor on the radio, too. You just never know about people. Bess said she used to love Woody Allen movies until the scandal with his little stepdaughter. I remember we had quite a discussion about whether the personal life of an artist should affect the way you feel about his art. (I should say "his or her" art, but it's hardly ever the women that can't control themselves.) It was the same for sports because we agreed we'd feel differently about players—no matter how good they were—if they got into trouble off the field. Even though Bess liked watching sports, she only liked to watch the teams she considered her home team: any University of Washington team, sometimes the Cougars, Gonzaga basketball, the Seattle Storm, Seahawks, OL Reign, and the Sounders. She didn't watch the Seattle Kraken ice hockey team because she couldn't see where the puck went. She thought they should have a bigger one. But I'd watch any team from anywhere—college or pro. I liked the conclusiveness of sports, especially now with the video in baseball where you can see if the guy was safe or out. You win or you lose. That's it. Game over. Not like life itself, which as it plays out is a mixed bag and seems to me more like the weather which can be all over the place and then change in a second, and then change back, or change to something else. So you never know what the score is or who's on first, which is how it is with me a lot of the time.

It was the middle of the fifth inning when Eddie knocked on the door of my bedroom and came in. "I heard the TV so I knew you were awake." Eddie was grinning. "While you were in here we got two more bookings!"

"You're kidding. We don't even have any reviews up yet."

"I guess it didn't matter to these people."

"Who are they?" I picked up the remote and turned down the volume.

"Two women from Portland next week. And after that, a woman from Seattle. Pretty great, I'd say."

"Frankly, I won't believe this whole thing until we see the money."

"You know what's the matter with you, George?"

"I'm not going to ask, because you'll tell me anyway."

"You don't have a positive attitude. You don't have faith."

I considered again mentioning to Eddie about his faith that people would want to sit in a lawn chair attached to helium balloons to ride up in the air, but that would be mean and Bess wouldn't like it, so I kept it to myself.

We heard Scottie's truck pull up and I turned off the game (which didn't bother me because the Mariners were losing) and I went with Eddie to let him in. As soon as Eddie opened the door Scottie burst in singing.

*"If a body meet a body ... Comin' thro the rye ... If
a body kiss a body ... Need a body cry ..."*

His jacket was open and he was dressed in a red plaid
kilt and he had a Scottish tam on his head. It was a
pointy thing with a red, black and white checked border
along the bottom, a little red pom-pom on the top, and
a couple of black ribbon streamers. I had been trying to
accept that Eddie had asked him to sing for our guests,
and of course, I never actually thought he'd wear his
tan coveralls with Scottie's Septic Magic written across
the back, but this was ridiculous. Not only was this
Airbnb thing not supposed to be a restaurant, but it
wasn't a dinner theater with a guy in a costume. Why
was this guy with fat dimpled knees and hairy legs
standing in the middle of my living room? I was losing
my grasp of the whole thing.

"Wow! You sure look the part," Eddie said as he
closed the door.

"I *am* the part," Scottie said with authority.

I just stared at him wondering if his legs got cold.

"It's a tartan, a Royal Stewart tartan." Scottie hung
up his jacket on the rack next to the door and walked
over to the fireplace and put his hand on the mantle,
posing for us in the outfit.

Eddie looked at the kilt. "Is anything worn under
there?"

"Worn? Everything's in perfect working order!" He
said, and laughed his head off.

"Ha ha ha!" Eddie cracked up and then he said,
"Scottie—this is going to be great because these guests
have an Irish name—they'll love you."

"I'm not Irish." He scowled and crossed his arms over his chest.

"Irish—Scottish, they're all Celts, what's the difference?"

"There's a difference!"

It was clear that Eddie, in his ignorance of culture and geography, typical of many Americans (myself included, I'm sorry to admit) was getting Scottie very annoyed. I wondered if he might leave and forget the whole thing, which would be fine from my standpoint. But Eddie was clueless and determined to please the O'Grady's whom he was sure would treasure their Irish roots no matter how many generations removed from Ireland they were. It never occurred to him that Cathy O'Grady might not even be Irish. Maybe she just had her husband's name and could be anything.

"Do you know any Irish songs?" he asked eagerly.

"I'm Scottish! Do you want me or not?"

But then I started to feel bad for the guy, which surprised me since I'd never wanted him in the first place. But he'd obviously gone to a lot of trouble to put on the outfit which looked very clean and freshly pressed and I was sure that, like most people in the arts, he couldn't make a living doing what he loved. The septic business was just to keep him afloat (even though he tried to elevate it by calling it Septic Magic). Clearly, his heart was in music.

"We want you, Scottie," I said quietly and what really surprised me was that I meant it. I looked at him standing there in his kilt and tam and realized I admired him. He'd moved to the island, a new place for him, and was here trying to create a new life for himself—starting a business and trying to get gigs around town. I couldn't have done that. True, I was embarking on something new with this business with Eddie. But it was all Eddie's doing. I was just going along, the way I had so much of my life.

"I wonder where the O'Grady's are?" Eddie looked at his watch, then picked up the phone to see if there were any messages. "They should be here by now if they got the 3:30 boat. It's almost 5:00. Maybe the boat was late and they stopped to have dinner or something. But wouldn't they call to let us know?"

"It's not like they're friends who feel like they should check in with us," I reminded him.

Bess used to say the island was ruled by the ferry gods. Everyone who lives here, as well as anyone who wants to come here, is at their mercy because Vashon has no bridge and you can only get here by boat or plane. And the ferries are not always reliable which can make getting to Seattle or Tacoma a hassle, but Eddie and I did it for years. In fact, over half the island, about five thousand people, are commuters. For those that do it, the beauty of the island, the quiet, the rural charm and the small town sense of community makes the aggravation of ferry dependence worth it. But it requires patience, and those who don't have it don't last long here.

"I'm sure they'll get here eventually, and whenever they get here, we're in good shape—the room is perfect and I've got food ready for their room so we don't have to do anything at the last minute," Eddie said.

"What food did you get?"

"Cheese, Ritz crackers and—"

"Why not Triscuits?"

"If you were so set on them you should have told me, George. But I got Fig Newtons, which are perfect because you have a fruit, with the fig so nicely tucked inside the pastry—all in one. Kind of like a corn dog is a complete meal."

"That's ridiculous. A corn dog doesn't have corn. There's no vegetable in there."

"Well, let's not argue about it. I'll take the food down to their room—so it'll be there when they get here." Eddie went to the kitchen and put everything on a tray and took it to the basement.

"I can wait for them, no problem," Scottie sounded quite cheerful. "I don't have any other gigs tonight. I'll just practice my songs."

"I guess I'll go watch the Mariners." I went back in my bedroom and turned on the game. It was now the eighth inning and the M's were still behind. I closed the door, but even with it closed I could hear Scottie practicing his songs.

"Ev'ry lassie has a laddie ...Nane, they sa'e ha'e I ..."

For Scottie's sake, and I suppose Eddie's, too, I hoped now that the O'Grady's would show up. It was the top of ninth when Eddie ran into my room.

"They're here! They're here!" Eddie was so excited he was like a little kid who thought Santa and a bunch of reindeers had landed on the roof. I looked out the window and saw a blue Volvo park behind Eddie's truck. It almost surprised me that it wasn't the Mercedes that had lodged in my brain.

"Oh no, where's the key?" Eddie looked around

frantically. "We have to give them the key! That's the first thing you do when the guests arrive."

"I'll get it."

"Okay, when they come in, I'll take their luggage and you give them the key and I'll show them to the room."

"Luggage? They're not staying for a month, Eddie."

"It's a courtesy, part of our excellent service."

In the living room Scottie was posed by the fireplace and I went to the desk to get the key. The minute Eddie heard them at the door, he flung it open.

Bob wasn't what I pictured at all. I thought he would look like Steve Jobs, but he was a round bald guy and looked like Elmer Fudd. He was wearing a dark blue puffy vest and baggy jeans. Cathy was dressed exactly the same: jeans, but with a powder blue vest. She was so skinny she looked like one of those pipe-cleaner figures we made when we were kids; she was bony and frail looking and her brassy blonde hair with its dark roots gave her a bizarre skeletal look that made me think of Halloween.

"Welcome to Bluebell Nook!" Eddie practically shouted.

Scottie took that as his cue and burst into song.

"Ev'ry lassie has her laddie ... Nane, they say, ha'e I,
Yet a' the lads they smile on me,
When comin' thro' the rye."

The O'Grady's stared at us like we were an accident on the freeway and I looked at Scottie and drew my finger across my neck, motioning him to cut the song. I walked over to Bob and handed him the key, "I'm

George," I said, introducing myself and held out my hand. Bob and I shook hands and then Cathy and I shook hands. They still looked stunned and Eddie ran over to them and introduced himself, shook hands with each of them and then motioned to Scottie. "This is Scottie who will entertain us over drinks."

I brought the appetizers and wine from the kitchen and put it on the table in front of the fireplace while Eddie pushed the O'Grady's over in front of the food where they caved, crumpled on the couch.

Scottie smiled at the O'Grady's. "Here's a favorite of mine," he said and then sang,

> *"Will ye go lassie go … And we'll all go together …*
> *To pluck wild mountain thyme … All around the*
> *blooming heather … Will ye go lassie go …"*

I started to open the wine but Cathy was hunched over holding her head, groaning.

"Hold it! We're exhausted." Bob jumped up. "We just want to go to our room."

Cathy looked up, still holding her head. "We were stuck in the ferry line for hours! I have a horrible headache."

I put the wine bottle down. "We're very sorry."

"Can we get you anything?" Eddie asked.

"Just our room!" Bob was shouting now.

Cathy stood up and they both picked up their bags. Eddie charged over to her. "Here let me help you." He pulled the bag away from her and she yanked it back from him and caught him off balance and he fell into her causing her to fall back on the couch.

"Oh my God. Let me out of here!"

Bob looked down at her sprawled on the couch and said between clenched teeth, as his jaw twitched, "We can't find anything else, Cathy we *have* to stay here."

"I'll show you to your room, just follow me." I didn't pick up the bags. Cathy was now clutching hers to her chest, and Bob gripped his like he was a Brinks security guard carrying a bag from a bank.

They followed me outside around the path to the door to the basement. We didn't say a word. They were both upset and I was not about to make friendly chit-chat about the weather, or ask where they were from or was this their first time to the island? Besides, chit-chat really wasn't my thing anyway. At the door to their room, I gave them the key and told them to be sure and let us know if they needed anything. They just glared at me, hurried in the room, and firmly shut the door.

Eddie didn't seem too bothered when I got back. "Did you show them the food I put out?"

"No, they just ran in the room and practically slammed the door." I went to the kitchen and got a glass of water. I was feeling light-headed and my mouth was dry. Bess always told me to be sure and drink enough water, she'd say "old people can easily get dehydrated, George." I thought the water would make me feel better—I drank a full glass, but when I went back to the living room I still felt crappy. It wasn't mysterious: not only did I have complete strangers in my basement, but they were totally pissed off.

"It was a rocky start, but when they see the food, they'll feel better," Eddie said, with conviction.

Scottie arranged his kilt around him as he sat in the plaid chair. "It's always good to eat a little something."

Seeing his plaid kilt against the orange and brown plaid chair almost made me dizzy. "She said she had a headache and wanted to sleep," I reminded them.

"In my experience food can help," Eddie said.

"I don't know about that." I went back to the kitchen for more water. "When I have a headache I don't want anything."

"I know the perfect thing," Scottie jumped up from the plaid chair and scurried over to stand in front the fireplace. "I'll sing a lullaby. It will be soothing and lovely. And just this once, I'll make an exception and sing an Irish lullaby. He didn't wait for us say anything, he immediately started in.

"Too ra loo ra loo ral …" he sang, *"Too ra loo ra li …*
Too ra loo ra loo ra … Hush now don't you cry …"

There was a loud thumping sound and Scottie stopped singing.

"What's that?" I stood up and looked around.

"It's from the basement ceiling," Scottie grinned, "it's applause! They want more—I'll sing louder!

"Too ra loo ra loo ral," *Too ra loo ra li …*
Too ra loo ra loo ral … That's an Irish lullaby…Over
in Killarney … Many year—"

"SHUT THE HELL UP!" Bob yelled, as he flung open the front door and charged over to us, "We're trying to sleep for God's sake!"

Eddie immediately apologized, "We're very sorry, sir. We thought the lullaby would help your wife."

"It's Irish," Scottie muttered.

"Help? It's making her sick!"

His wife looked pretty sickly to me to begin with, I thought. But of course, I couldn't say that. But I did wish I could think of something helpful to say that would calm him down. Some people have that gift. They know just what to say to people who are upset, scared or angry—they're great when there's a lot of tension or a crisis of some kind. The right words just naturally come to them. Bess was like that. But not yours truly. I was lousy at small talk, so to think of reassuring words in a situation like this—a stranger coming up from my basement, furious about a guy in a kilt singing and tormenting his wife—was more than just being out of my wheelhouse. It was out of my total range as a human being, such as playing first base for the Yankees, winning a Noble Prize for anything, or conducting the New York Philharmonic.

Just then, as I was mired in the quicksand of my complete inadequacy, we heard a high-pitched scream—and a second later, like thunder following lightning: *"It's HORRIBLE! I can't stand it here!"*

"Oh my God! Now what!" Bob threw up his hands and tore back down to the basement.

"My singing wasn't that bad," Scottie muttered, as he walked over to the door. He yanked his coat from the rack, and then left without saying another word.

Eddie usually has an answer for everything, but as we heard Scottie's truck start up and drive away, Eddie seemed off his game. We just stood in the middle of the room looking at each other. Then Bob stormed back in and glared at us.

"A big fat mouse ran out of the shower! We can't book anywhere else tonight, but we demand a full refund," he growled.

"What about the food?" Eddie said, politely. I had to hand it to him—he sure bounced back fast.

"Velveeta cheese and Fig Newtons ... you call that food! And there's no view—the website said there was a view of Colvos passage!"

"You just go up the hill behind the house and you can see it. It's a very pretty view." Eddie didn't sound rattled at all.

"I'm writing a review warning people about this place!" Bob started to leave, but Eddie stopped him.

"How 'bout a full refund, plus $50 not to write the review?"

"$100." Bob glared at him.

"$75." Eddie countered.

"Okay, a full refund plus $75 not to write the review. But it better be quiet the rest of the night or the deal's off," he snapped, then headed back to the basement.

Eddie and I tiptoed to the kitchen, opened the refrigerator and took out a couple of beers. I sat in the plaid chair and Eddie sat across from me on the couch. Eddie didn't say anything and just drank his beer. He seemed deep in thought.

I took a swig of my beer, then said quietly, "Guess we struck out with O'Grady's."

He was quiet for a while, then he set his beer on the coffee table and leaned forward with his hands on his knees. "Next time I think we should get better cheese," he said. "And also offer a little extra something—like a little dab of Cheez-Whiz."

THE HUMANE TRAP

THERE WAS NO GETTING AROUND IT. THE LAUNCH OF Bluebell Nook was a disaster, but Eddie, true to his nature, was as optimistic as ever. We had two bookings coming up (the two women from Portland and after that the Seattle woman) and Eddie, cheerful and undaunted, was convinced they'd absolutely love staying with us and everything would come up roses.

That unshakeable faith was hard for me to relate to, much less understand. It's not like we were Oscar and Felix, those guys from *The Odd Couple*. We were alike in a lot of ways, both kind of messy and not too particular about much of anything. In fact, the only reason Eddie was motivated to tidy up my house was because he wanted the business to succeed. Both of our trucks were grubby, which was reflective of much of the island's culture when it came to cleanliness standards for vehicles. In fact, in all the years I've lived here I've never once seen a car or truck where someone had written "Wash Me" in its dirt. When it came to our truck's interiors, it was a tossup which of our trucks was the biggest mess. In terms of our interests, we both liked to fish, watch sports (except for Nascar, which we argued about and I will never consider a sport) and drink a few beers. Overall, Eddie and I were generally down-to-earth guys. Live-and-let-live was pretty much the way we operated in the world. But there was one big difference: Eddie was a risk taker and I wasn't. He always believed things would work out for the best. Not me. In fact, if it had totally been up to me, I would have bailed on Bluebell Nook. It would not have taken much for me to get up the nerve to cancel our upcoming reservations. Having those O'Grady people screaming at us and having to pay them was all the motivation I needed. I suggested as much to Eddie.

"I'll even call the two women from Portland and the one from Seattle," I offered.

"And what would you tell them?"

"I might say there'd been a horrible mudslide that left slimy sludge all over the house so we'd have to cancel."

"And what if they wanted to re-book in a few months?" He sounded like a prosecutor.

"I could say there's been a fire in the chimney, or I know—better than that, an infestation of red ants. No one would be willing to come after that. They'd always imagine lying in bed in the Airbnb afraid of ants crawling all over them. Once that idea is in your head it's hard to shake it."

"Look, George—I know it could have gone better with the O'Gradys—"

"Gone better! Are you kidding me? It was a friggin' disaster!"

"So, it's one strike and we're out? Is that it?"

"Why not? Why set ourselves up for having one little mouse make a guest go ballistic? There's mice all over the place—this is a rural area. Rural areas have mice. Why set ourselves up for all this hassle!"

Eddie was quiet for a long time, which made me nervous. It wasn't like him. Eddie always has something to say. But he just stared at me until finally he said, "You promised you'd give it a month."

Well, that got me. If the situation had been reversed, even though he's flaky about a lot of things, I've always known I could count on Eddie to do what he says. That's one of his good qualities. And when I think of myself, in spite of the fact that it's usually a stretch for me to think of any of my good qualities, I do see myself as being reliable. Being a man of my word. So as much I was ready to see Bluebell Nook find its place in the graveyard of stupid business ventures, and as much as it pained me, I said, "Look, I was just trying to convince you to change your mind about it. But if you still want to go through with it—"

"I do."

"Well, okay then. That's it, we'll give it a month."

"And do our best."

Eddie looked so worried that I felt bad, so I told him I'd look into getting mousetraps and that seemed to cheer him up.

It seemed like a fool's errand because everyone on the island has trouble with mice and even rats and no matter what you do the little buggers always find a way to get in. The worst is when they eat the wires of your car. But I had been lucky that never happened to me. Maybe my truck wires weren't that tasty. But I went to get traps anyway and I have to say I was surprised at how many mouse traps they had at the hardware store. I ended up getting one that was called CaptSure Upgraded Humane Smart Mouse Trap. I wondered why they called it a smart mouse trap. Was it because the trap was smart, as opposed to a stupid mouse trap? Or was it to trap smart mice and not stupid ones? It wasn't electronic like smart phones, so I thought the name didn't really fit and on the box it said it was 100% cruelty free, which I thought made sense because there were people who wanted to make sure they didn't buy a cruel trap. You were supposed to put the bait inside a plastic tube and when the mouse ran in to get it, the weight of the mouse would cause the door to shut behind it and it would be stuck inside. Then you were supposed to humanely take it outside (hopefully not near someone else's house) and humanely let it run wild and free. I set the trap with some of the leftover Velveeta and I hoped the mouse would find it more appealing than the O'Gradys had.

After I the set the trap, I went down to Baker's Beach to see Martha Jane. It was early afternoon when I got to her house and she greeted me in her bathrobe, which worried me. More than that, to be honest—I was a little alarmed.

"Are you okay? Not feeling well?" I tried to hide how concerned I was.

"Oh no, honey. I'm fine. I figured I knew you well enough now. Come on in. You see George, there are just some days that it's too much trouble to get dressed. Like today when it's gray and the rain is expected all day. I don't plan on going anywhere, I'll mostly read and nap a bit, so staying in my pajamas seems quite the right thing to do."

"A very good thing," I agreed, feeling relieved and I followed her to the kitchen. It made me happy to be in her kitchen, it always smelled good, even when she hadn't been cooking anything. It was hard to identify it, just a very nice smell—close to vanilla, but not exactly vanilla. It was a stark difference from the old bachelor smell of my house, which still permeated every corner in spite of Eddie's efforts to spruce everything up for the business.

Martha Jane sat at the table and the cat jumped in her lap. "I'd often be in my bathrobe when Bess and I had our tea, and so today I just thought, why not with you?"

"I'm glad I've passed the test." I smiled and went to the counter. We had a routine now. She had the hot water ready, the mugs and tea bags laid out, and I'd fix the tea and then bring it to the table.

"Well, I'm glad you see it that way. I'm not sure why being in your pajamas all day would generally be frowned on, anyway. Maybe it's assumed you're lazy and decadent. But you're very understanding and accepting, George. You know those are two of the three most important things a person can give someone," she said, taking a sip of her tea.

"Really? What's the third?"

She was quiet for a minute. "I forget …"

"Well, two seems enough."

"I usually don't worry if I can't remember things. Why fret about it? That just takes energy. And since I don't have as much energy as I used to, I don't like to use it on stupid things ..."

"That makes a lot of sense."

"... oh, I remember now ... the third thing is encouragement. That's it. The three most important things one person can give another are understanding, acceptance and encouragement. But not to unrealistically encourage someone, like telling a person who is selling vegetables at a farm stand that they're going to make millions."

"That's hardly anything to worry about with me. I'm afraid I usually see the glass half empty."

She smiled and folded her hands together and leaned forward. "So how did it go? When you told me the name you chose, I thought it was great. Bluebell something wasn't it?"

"Nook. Bluebell Nook."

"Oh, right. Lovely name. It makes me think of a beautiful fresh meadow and nook is just a wonderful cozy concept. Like curling up with a book in a window seat."

"I wish." I shook my head and looked at the raindrops dripping down the window. Finally, I just told her. "There's no way to get around it, Martha Jane. We couldn't be off to a worse start. We had our first guests and it was awful." And I proceeded to explain about the O'Grady's and how we ended up having to pay them.

"You paid *them*?"

"I'm afraid so. Eddie negotiated the price—a full refund, plus $75 not to write a bad review. The whole thing was a failure."

"There's a saying that success is going from failure to failure without losing your enthusiasm. Maybe that's a definition of success that fits Eddie."

"Probably does. You know I wonder sometimes what is it that makes it so easy for some people to take risks."

Out the window there wasn't much wind, the leaves on the trees next to the house were still, and rain was softly falling on the beach and pebbling the silvery mirror of the water across the cove. A seagull was perched on a driftwood log; he didn't seem to be doing much of anything and I thought he looked very content. He probably had a pretty good life since he could just stand around like that. The gray cement sky was quite a contrast to Martha Jane's sunny yellow kitchen. It was warm and cozy with Martha Jane in her bathrobe and the two of us sipping our tea and I wondered if I could ever arrive at a place of such confidence and contentment that I could happily stay in my bathrobe all day. I think Bess would say that it would be a sign of spiritual progress.

"I'm not sure why some take risks and others don't. It's a mystery," she said, "maybe it's just that some creatures are born more timid than others. All you have to do is take a look at a litter of puppies. I'm sure you've seen them—the adventurous ones that explore everything and tumble around and pounce on their siblings, and those that stay huddled next to their mother and don't venture out as much. And little kids—same thing. The ones on the playground that hang upside down on the jungle gym, and the ones off in a corner carefully making mud pies. And when it comes to adults, my observation is that the ones who can take risks are able to see the endeavor as a separate thing from the core of who they are as a human being. So if it fails, it's the project that didn't work, but their humanity, the essence of who they are remains intact."

I wondered about when you failed another person. Could you still keep that separate from the core of who you are as a human being? When you let other people down? Or were hurtful? I was tempted to ask her ... but I didn't.

Martha Jane stroked her cat who began to purr. "I never saw Maria when she was a kitten. I adopted her from our shelter on the island when she was about six months old. She was a great mouser when she was younger, so I suspect she'd been a pretty adventurous kitten."

"It was a mouse that freaked out our guest. She went ballistic."

"That's too bad. I don't know why some people get so upset. Although I've always heard elephants have a problem with mice."

"I set a humane trap this morning. After the mouse goes in the trap you're supposed to just let it out somewhere and not kill it. I just hope we get rid of them before the next person is supposed to come. Eddie and I realized it wasn't a good idea to leave the food out in the guest's room and he ordered a mini refrigerator from Amazon. We tried to get one on the island, but couldn't find one. Eddie and I agreed on that—always trying the island first. And that's how Bess and I were, we always tried to support island business."

"I'm like that, too. We won't have them if we don't." She lifted her glasses that had slid down her nose. "Isn't that true of most things? That we won't have them if we don't support them. I still keep thinking about

Woody—that he probably didn't have support from anyone. Although of course, I don't really know that."

It took me a while to remember that Woody was the name she gave the dead guy. "Did you call the county again?"

She nodded. "I did. But no one has claimed him."

She slowly started to get up, but I put my hand on hers. "I can get it. More tea, right?"

"Yes, thanks." She sat back down. "You know George, I don't normally think of myself as a superstitious type, or one that believes much in signs and omens."

"No, you seem very practical to me." I poured her tea and brought it to the table.

"But I keep thinking about why was I the one to discover Woody? Was I suppose to help in some way? Is there some meaning to his washing up right here on our beach? I feel compelled to do something about him, although I don't know what it is. I've even been thinking that I should have a memorial service for him. Of course I know nothing about him, so I don't know what it should be. It's has me kind of flummoxed."

Martha Jane wasn't one to ever get too rattled by things. But this business with the dead guy, with Woody, it was bothering her. I wished I could come up with something to say that would be helpful and reassuring. Bess would have known. Bess always knew what to say to make people feel better. It was her nature—I think she was just born with it. I closed my eyes, then looked at the beach again. The rain hadn't let up and the seagull was still there, standing on the driftwood.

Just tell her it will work out.

But will it?

It usually does, George. And even if it doesn't, it can't hurt to think it will until you have to face whatever comes next.

I gazed out at the rain for a minute and then turned back and looked across the table. "I'm sure it will work itself out, Martha Jane."

"Do you think so?"

"I do," I said, and when I saw her smile, I believed it. I just wished I could apply that to me. The next guests would be coming soon. Two women. Two more strangers in my house. And I was dreading it.

THE LADY FROM PORTLAND

The rest of that week I didn't see much of Eddie. He was spending a lot of time helping Lottie. She'd thrown her back out changing sheets in her beach house. A lot of people who had Airbnbs hired cleaners to change the sheets and clean the bathrooms, but Lottie didn't want to spend the money. She said she didn't want anything to cut into her profits and had been doing all the work herself—that is, until her back went out. And Eddie was happy to oblige. He took care of Max for her, feeding him, walking him a couple of times a day and he cleaned her beach house after the guests left. He actually seemed to be spending more time at Happy Isle Hideaway than he was at Bluebell Nook, which was fine with me. It was quieter and I could see that it meant something to Eddie to be needed over at Lottie's. And I had to admit, that as much as I was not looking forward to more guests, getting the basement ready for our next guests gave me something to do besides feeding the chickens. The next ones were supposed to be the two women from Portland, but we got a call from one of the women to say that her friend wasn't able to come. Eddie was at Lottie's so I took the call.

"Bluebell Nook." This was how I answered the phone now, instead of just saying 'hello.'

"Hi, this is Molly Gorman—"

"Hello."

"I'm calling because we have reservations for the 14th, but my friend isn't able to come—

(Oh good.)

—and I'll be coming by myself and wonder if I could come a day early?"

(Why come at all? You won't like it here.)

"Hello? Are you there?"

"Yeah, okay—that would be fine." (Not really.)

"Great, thanks. I'll be there on the 13th."

Right after we hung up I wondered if I was supposed to say that it wouldn't cost as much since there was now just one person. But then I wondered if she would have initiated mentioning a reduced rate if that was the expected thing? Or maybe it was like when a restaurant totally screws up your order so they offer to take something off the bill. It's just understood that they'll offer to do that and the customer doesn't need to ask for it. (That happened to us one time at a restaurant in Tacoma. Bess ordered halibut and when it came it was a dried up thing like a block of white packing material and we didn't have to pay, which I thought was appropriate.) I have to say, I lack entrepreneurial instincts, I didn't need anything like that all those years at Boeing. Lottie would know about this sort of thing, but I didn't want to bother her with her back and all, so I just let it go. Another thing I let go was Scottie. I didn't call him to have him come and sing for the lady. I thought it was a lot simpler to get out of the entertainment business and Eddie wasn't around to object.

The week between the O'Grady's and the arrival of the next guest, I'd caught two mice in the basement guest room. Bess would have approved of that Capt-Sure Upgraded Humane Smart Mouse Trap because it really was 100% cruelty free. Unlike a lot of things you buy where the hype and all the advertising turns out to be just a bunch of b.s., the little mice were unharmed inside the plastic tube. They must have run in the trap at the exact same time, side by side, so the door of the trap closed on the two of them. I took the trap with the mice stuck inside a long way from the house—at least over a hundred yards until I got to the forest. I went in among the trees and set it down next to some huge ferns at the base of a fir tree. Then I opened the trap door to let them out. The first little guy scurried right out, but the other one stayed in the back. Maybe he or she was hoping for more Velveeta. Or maybe it was just stupid. I waited a few minutes, but it just sat there so I picked up the tube and bent over close to the ground and turned it upside down and dumped it out. I wanted to dump it close to the ground because if it was too high I didn't know if it would get hurt. Maybe they didn't have nine lives like cats.

After I humanely released the mice into the forest, I went back to the house to get the room ready for the Portland lady. I dusted, vacuumed and mopped the bedroom and then I got pissed off. Why did I ever think I wouldn't mind Eddie being over at Lottie's, leaving me with all this? Why should I be cleaning the bathroom, scrubbing everything including the toilet by myself? What a chump. Not only did I not want to keep going with this dumb business—I just agreed because I promised Eddie—but now he wasn't even here. He should at least come over and pitch in with the bathroom and the other stuff to get ready for the lady who I didn't even want to come—so I called him.

"Eddie, listen—"

"Hi George, everything okay?"

"No."

"What's wrong?"

"I'm not doing this crap myself."

"What crap, George?"

"Cleaning the damn room, Eddie! And the bath-room—we're supposed to do this together!"

"Lottie really needs the help."

"She should pay someone then, she's just too cheap."

"Bill left her with a lot of debts, it's not like she's rolling in dough."

"I'm not calling about Lottie's finances. Can't she spare you for an hour to get over here and pull your own oar, Eddie?"

"I guess I could ask her—"

"Ask her? You need her permission? Listen, Eddie I heard the TV in the background. What's going on on over there?"

"Lottie likes the shopping channel. It's on most of the time."

"So she can buy stuff, instead of paying someone to work there?"

"She's really hurting, George. Her back is messed up."

"Okay, okay—just try to get over here for a little while," I said, and hung up.

Eddie came over not long after that and helped me clean the bathroom (he did the toilet and I did the sink and shower). Then we washed the towels and sheets, put up fresh towels and new fancy soap, and made the bed with the other set of clean sheets. He worked hard; he's a lot faster than I am and he does a good job, so I didn't stay mad. I told him I could do the rest and he should go back to Lottie's. When I thought about it, I felt sad for Lottie. I messed up my back once when I was hauling cement blocks to shore up our carport and it was some serious pain, so I did get it. Eddie drives me nuts, but he's basically a good guy and it was clear he was worried about Lottie and wanted to help her. I don't think he intentionally had been trying to weasel out of work at Bluebell Nook. At least I hoped not.

After he left I put some grapes, a bottle of white wine from one of the island wineries and some cheddar cheese from a local farm in the mini refrigerator, the one Eddie had gotten from Amazon. I also set a bottle of cabernet on the table near the door, so everything was all set for the Portland lady.

We'd been having typical spring weather with a mix of cloudy days, partially sunny days, days of all rain, and some days with a little of every thing. But the night the woman from Portland came there was nothing tentative or ambivalent about the weather. It was pouring down rain. Raining cats and dogs as they say. One time Bess looked up where that expression came from and she learned that in England, a long time ago, although I can't remember how long, cats and dogs used to sleep on the roof and when it rained they would slide off the roof. Bess was curious like that. But I was never quite sure about that because I could understand that cats might climb on a roof, but I didn't understand how dogs would get there. That part never made sense to me.

I looked around the living room and everything looked pretty clean and tidy. As much as I didn't want another guest, I didn't want to do a half-assed job. I'm not sure if it was because I'd promised Eddie, which meant I'd try to do my best, or if Bess would want me not to screw it up. Maybe a bit of both. The rain was pounding against the windows and the house was pretty damp so I decided to make a fire. I went to the fireplace and opened the screen, crouched down and started putting kindling in when I heard a knock on the door. I guess I hadn't heard a car because the rain was so loud. It took me a minute to stand up, my knees were objecting, and as I hurried to the door I heard the knock again and swung open the door just as the woman was about to knock again.

"This is Bluebell Nook?" she asked. She wore a dark blue Columbia rain parka and was drenched just from coming the distance between the car and the house. The parka had the hood up and I couldn't see her face too well.

"Hi, yes—I'm sorry I didn't hear you knock at first—I was just trying to get a fire started. Please come in." After she came in, I shut the door behind her and asked, "Can I take your coat?" I wasn't sure if this was the right thing to say. I think because basically the Airbnb concept was confusing to me. Sometimes it seemed like it was just a motel room only in your house, and all you were supposed to do was give the people the key and then they'd go to the room and that would be the end of it. But then there was the bed and breakfast idea, the B & B thing, where the owners were friendly and treated the customers more like their house guests. This woman had come here in the dark all by herself and it was chilly and wet, and I knew Bess would say I should ask if she'd like something to drink. And I was just about to do that when she held out her hand and introduced herself.

"I'm Molly Gorman, by the way."

"Oh, sorry. I'm George," I said, as we shook hands. "George Beasley." I hung up her coat on the rack next to the door. "It sure is coming down tonight."

"Good weather for ducks," she said, with a big laugh. I wasn't sure why that was funny until I saw that she was wearing a green Oregon sweatshirt with the Ducks logo. She had very short white hair that framed her face in little silvery-white points and didn't seem to have on any make-up that I could tell. She had a stocky, athletic build and I wondered if she'd ever played a sport for Oregon. I've noticed that the shapes of most women— and men, too, for that matter, look kind of settled when they get old with their bodies getting kind of blobby. And I thought she did look about my age, except she looked sturdy and not settled and blobby.

"Would you like something to drink?"

"I was just going to ask for the key," she said,

smiling at me, "but I wouldn't mind something to drink, thanks."

"I can make coffee or tea, and we have wine if you'd like."

"Wine would be great. Something to warm me up."

"Just have a seat and I'll bring you a glass." I gestured to the couch. "Then I can get the fire going. My partner Eddie is usually here, but he can't be here tonight. So it's just me."

I went to get the wine and thought maybe I shouldn't have told her that. Maybe that would make her uneasy, being alone in a strange house with a strange man.

I looked all around the kitchen but I couldn't find any wine. We'd had a few bottles and I'd taken a white one and a red one to the basement, but there should have been at least one more. Eddie and I usually just drink beer, and then it occurred to me that he'd probably taken some wine over to Lottie's. I went back in the living room. "Um, I'm sorry I thought we had wine, but there is some in your room. It's in the basement. I could run down and bring it back up. Or we have beer ..."

"A beer would be great. No need to go out in this rain if you don't have to."

"It's not Henry's."

"Pardon?"

"Henry Weinhard."

She laughed, "Ah, Oregon's great beer. Anything's fine, really."

I went back to the kitchen and got a couple of Budweisers. I reminded myself that both Eddie and Bess would tell me to put it in a glass so I got two glasses from the cupboard. I thought I should offer some food, but I'd taken the cheese and grapes to the basement and I was sure she'd say not to go down to get that. I poured the beer in the glasses and looked around for the Triscuits, but Eddie and I had eaten most of the stuff we'd had for the O'Grady's.

"It's Budweiser," I said, as I handed her the beer. "And I'm afraid we don't have much of anything to eat to go with it."

"Thanks. I like Budweiser and don't worry about food. I came early, so I wouldn't expect you to be all that ready."

"There might be a few Fig Newtons and some Velveeta cheese, but that's about it, I'm sorry."

"Fig Newtons? Velveeta?" She grinned. "Really?"

"I don't suppose you'd want any of that." I sat down across from her. I took a big gulp of the beer and then sat in the plaid chair and started poking the stuffing in the hole of the arm.

"I haven't had either of those in years." She gave me a big smile. "It reminds me of my childhood—stuff like Jello, canned peaches, Spam." She laughed. "Why not? Let's have some."

"Really?" I couldn't help being surprised. "Well, okay—coming right up."

I got up and went to the kitchen and I found a half-eaten package of Fig Newtons. I took one out of the package and bit into it; it seemed a little stale, but not too bad, so I put the rest of them on a plate. It would be nicer than just bringing out the half-eaten package. And I cut the Velveeta into little strips to make it look more attractive and put them around the Fig Newtons.

As I set the plate on the coffee table, I was still chewing the Fig Newton I had sampled.

"Very elegant," she said laughing and reached for a piece of Velveeta. "Yum."

My mouth was full of the Fig Newton, so I just nodded and then went to the fireplace to finish making the fire. She didn't seem to be that sarcastic about the food being elegant, it felt more like a fun teasing thing, like I was in on the joke, too.

"I was thinking about food I had as a kid and I had no idea Spam was a favorite Hawaiian food until I went to college and my roommate was from Honolulu. They have this snack in Hawaii called Spam musubi and it's grilled Spam on top of a little block of rice wrapped with seaweed. Kind of a Japanese Spam thing."

"Have you ever tasted it? The Hawaiian Spam thing?" I slid some fire starter sticks under the kindling and lit them in several places, and when the kindling was burning I set logs on top. After I made sure they'd caught, I went back to sit across from her.

"No, I guess I'm a purist when it comes to Spam," she said and laughed again. She had an easy laugh. "So, how long have you had Bluebell Nook?"

"It's brand new. We just opened it a couple of weeks ago. It was my partner Eddie's idea."

"And you and Eddie, you've been together a while?"

"We met over thirty years ago, we both worked at Boeing and made the commute together. We're retired now." It seemed odd, her asking how long Eddie and I had been together. As I poked the stuffing in the chair, it occurred to me maybe it was because I said he was my partner, so she thought we were gay. And then I thought she was probably gay because she was supposed to come with her friend and she wore that Ducks sweatshirt and looked athletic and had very short hair. And if she assumed I was gay, it was probably because she was gay because that would be why being gay would be in her mind.

"So you just opened—how's it going?"

"The Airbnb?"

She nodded and took a bite of a Fig Newton.

"Terrible." The minute I said that I knew I shouldn't have because you're not supposed to tell people when you're starting a business that things have been terrible. I know Eddie would have wanted to paint a glowing picture so the guest would feel that they were very fortunate to be staying in such a fabulous sought-after place. I don't know why I blurted that out. I guess there was just something about her that made you not want to lie or say something fake. Her face was kind and her eyes were open and curious. They were blue.

"Really? It's been terrible?" She took another Fig Newton.

"There was a mouse in the room and the lady freaked out. And we had a singer—"

"The Scottish singer? I saw that on your website—"

"Right. Well, they hated his singing. They wanted to sleep and we should have realized that, but it was the mouse that finally ruined it for them. But don't worry, I set a trap and caught two little guys and encouraged them to find a new home in the woods. Catch and release, as they say. Very humane. And I'm sure you won't be bothered by them."

"That is better than some of those traps. Like the

glue where their little feet get stuck. That's really awful."
She tipped the glass back and finished her beer. "But
really, there's not a lot that bothers me. I grew up on a
farm near Corvallis and I'm used to all kinds of creatures." She stretched and then yawned, covering her
mouth. "Well, I guess I better turn in," she said and
stood up.

"I'll get your key." I went to the kitchen and opened
the cupboard where we'd put a hook for the key. It was
Eddie's idea to always put it back on the hook so we
wouldn't misplace it. I handed her the key and told her
the path to the basement room was to the left. "Do you
have a bag or anything I can carry for you?"

"Oh, I just have a small carry-on in the car, but
thanks."

"The light by the path is pretty bright, you can
turn it off from the room if it's too bright. The switch
is right next to the door."

"Thanks, sounds good. And thanks for the beer and
the treats."

"Goodnight, Molly. Sleep well."

She smiled and I shut the door behind her. What a
nice woman.

But after I went to bed, I lay awake thinking how weird
it was that a strange woman was sleeping in my basement. I wondered if I would ever get used to this. I
kind of wished Eddie were here—I felt uneasy with just
me and Molly Gorman alone in the house, although
I'm not sure why. She seemed to like it here okay and
learning that we'd had mice didn't bother her. I don't

know what I was worried about. When I got up to go to the bathroom (something my old plumbing caused me to do quite a few times each night) from the window next to the sink I saw a glow in the yard coming from the lamp in the basement. She was probably reading. Bess always liked to read at night before she went to sleep. She worried that the light would bother me, she even offered to get one of those little lights that clip on a book, but I never minded. And when she closed the book, took off her glasses, put them on the bedside and turned off the light, I would reach for her.

Bess would never have married me if it hadn't been for Vince Kelly. So I owed him. Jerk that he was. Even though the University of Washington wasn't that far from the Braxton's house, it was an entirely separate place, a world unto itself. Bess lived in a dorm on campus and found it easy to avoid telling her parents anything about her social life; they knew what classes she was taking and who some of her girlfriends were, but that was about it. When it came to Vince, they were totally in the dark.

Vince had long since flunked out of the University and was renting a room in a house a few blocks from the campus. This meant Bess didn't have any need for me the way she had in high school when she'd sneak out and I'd cover for her. At first I worried that I'd never see her at the U—that we'd just go our separate ways. The school was huge, well over 30,000, and if you didn't have any classes together or live near each other on campus, you had to make an effort to get together.

And Bess did. She often wanted to meet for coffee, and I always wanted to see her, but I found it confusing. Being with Vince was easy for her now and she had some close girlfriends she trusted and could talk to— so I never could completely get my head around why she was spending time with me.

One afternoon when we were having coffee in the HUB she confided, "I'm afraid of the wild child in me. George, I know Vince is trouble and I've tried to break it off a few times, but he reels me back in somehow."

I wondered what it would be like to have that effect on a girl. I envied Vince for that. He could have the rest of his pathetic life, but the way he kept Bess coming back to him—I wanted that. But instead of just listening to her go on about Vince, and how conflicted she was, I got up the nerve to ask her something I'd wondered about ever since we'd been at college.

"Bess, do you still hang out with me because you feel sorry for me?"

"What?"

"You know, because of my mom and all." I'd never forgotten that day in the hospital when her father told my mother he'd take care of her boy. And Bess had been there, making the same promise.

"I love you, George." She lay her hand on my arm. I sucked in my breath and her eyes were so clear and true, like sea glass. And I stared at her, afraid to move. "You're like a brother to me. I'm surprised you don't know that."

I couldn't say anything at first. Finally, I looked away. "I know I'm good old George."

"I don't take you for granted, if that's what you're thinking. You're one of the most important people in my life. It surprises me, really—that you haven't seen that."

I guess there was no reason for me not to believe her. Maybe she did feel a certain kind of love for me. But it wasn't the same as what I felt. It wasn't equal. It wasn't reciprocal. I wanted to make love to her and she just wanted her head on my shoulder. But at least I knew I was important to her. I came to believe that, and it never had been so clear as it was that next summer when Vince was killed.

A NICE GUEST

IN THE MORNING I HAD JUST FINISHED FEEDING THE chickens when Molly came up the path from the basement. She was wearing jeans and a gray sweatshirt with a red logo for the Thorns, the Portland women's soccer team. She seemed very cheerful. She was walking briskly and greeted me with a wave and big smile. "Morning, George," she said. "Looks like it's going to be a beautiful day. I just love how fresh and clean it smells after a big rain, don't you?"

I took a big whiff of the fresh air. "Better today for sure, although we did need the rain." Weather seemed like the subject you should talk about with guests. I tried to think of what else to say, and then I realized Bess would want me to ask her how things were. "So, everything okay? You sleep okay?"

"The room is lovely and the bed is very comfortable, but I did have a little visitor this morning," she laughed.

"Oh no." I rubbed my head. "I'll put the trap down right away. I'm very sorry about this."

"It was kind of cute, it just ran across the room while I was getting dressed. It's always hard to tell how they get in. They really are little Houdinis."

"I'd hate to have the trap right there in the room

while you're there, that doesn't seem right. Are you going to be out for a while? I could put it down and hope we catch it before you come back."

"I was going to get some breakfast and then explore the island a bit. Can you recommend a good place to eat?"

"Well, Sporty's has giant pancakes and many people love it—"

"I just want some coffee and a little something. I'm not one for a big breakfast—"

Invite her in for coffee, George.

"Oh, well … I have coffee. Come on in and have a cup—"

"I don't want to trouble you."

Tell her you can make toast

"I can make toast."

and mention jam.

"And we have some very nice jam."

"Well, if you insist," she said with a smile. "That sounds perfect."

"I feel bad about the mouse—it's the least I can do."

In the kitchen I pulled out a chair for her. The table looked grubby so I grabbed a paper towel, got it wet and quickly wiped the table top as she was sitting down. Bess wouldn't want her to sit at a table that had goo stuck to it.

"Do you take anything in it?" I asked, as I poured the coffee.

"Just black, thanks."

"We only have whole wheat bread, is that okay?"

"Perfect." I handed her the coffee and she took a sip. "This is strong, just the way I like it."

In the refrigerator I found some plum jam that Martha Jane's neighbors, Howie and Mark, had given me, and I put that on the table with a plate and the butter dish. I wasn't sure if I should stay with her and keep her company. It was another one of those confusing things about how to act with a stranger that was paying to stay in your house. But I thought it was very important to take care of the mouse, so I got the trap from under the sink and put some more Velveeta in it.

"I'm going to take the trap down to your room, if that's okay?" I thought I should ask permission to go in the room, since it was her territory while she was staying here.

She buttered her toast and then put some jam on it. "That's fine, but don't worry if you don't catch it right away. It really doesn't bother me."

"Okay, I'll be back in a minute."

She certainly had a nice attitude—seemed like a very flexible person. What a contrast to that O'Grady woman. As I carried the trap down to the room, it surprised me to realize I didn't mind all that much having her here. It wasn't that bad. Not as terrible as I'd expected. As long as Eddie did his part of the work, it was possible this business could be tolerable if future guests were as easy as this one. And it wouldn't be half bad to have some extra money.

In the basement, I tried not to look around the room because it felt weird, like trespassing and snooping. But I couldn't help noticing her carry-on bag on the chair—the lid was open and there was a green plaid flannel nightgown draped over it. Bess had a flannel nightgown, it was blue plaid. Like a lot of her clothes, it came from L.L. Bean. She liked how warm and soft it was, especially in the winter. I felt stupid staring at this lady's nightgown, like I was peeking at something I shouldn't see. So I quickly put the mouse trap down near the bathroom door and left.

As I walked up the path from the basement, Eddie was coming back from Lottie's. He saw the blue Prius with the Oregon plates. "So, the women from Portland got here okay. Everything go all right?"

"Just the one came, her friend couldn't come. I hate to tell you—but there was another mouse in the room this morning."

"Oh no!"

"She was nice about it. I just set the trap again—she's inside having coffee. And I made toast for her."

"Good. She really didn't freak out?"

"Didn't seem to phase her. And I gave her jam with the toast."

"You're getting the hang of this, George. If you treat people right, they'll tell their friends and write a good review and like Lottie said, there's nothing more important than that."

"How's she doing?"

"Her back's enough better this morning that she felt up to walking Max and I got her beach house ready for the guests, so she said she didn't need me."

Eddie was telling me about all the good reviews Lottie got for Happy Isle Hideaway when Molly came out. She had on her parka and was holding her car keys. I waved her over and introduced her to Eddie.

"Nice to meet you," she said, shaking his hand. "You two sure have a beautiful spot here."

Eddie grinned. "Thanks, glad you think so." Then he looked concerned and lowered his voice, "George told me about the mouse. We're terribly sorry about that, and we're hoping to have it all taken care of soon."

"Not to worry, like I told George, I grew up on a farm so it's not a big deal for me." She laughed and went to her car. "I'm off to explore. See you guys, later." As she backed the car around she put down the window and yelled, "Thanks for the coffee and toast."

I gave her a thumbs up and she waved as she headed down the drive.

In the kitchen there was coffee left and I poured some for me and Eddie. I noticed Molly had cleared her dishes, rinsed them off and set them on the counter next to the sink. She didn't have to do that, she was paying us after all, but maybe it was force of habit. Or maybe she's as confused as I am about how to act with this Airbnb thing. Who knows?

"That woman from Oregon—"

"Molly ... Molly Gorman." I sipped my coffee.

"She sure is an improvement over that O'Grady woman."

"That's for sure."

"How did it go last night when she arrived?" he asked.

"It was pouring when she got here, so I made a fire and asked her in for a drink. We even ate the leftover Fig Newtons and the Velveeta, although I'm saving the rest for the mice. But she was easy to talk to, so it went fine."

"Good for you, like I said—you're really getting the hang of this."

"Bess always said she felt really close to her guy friends who are gay, like Howie and Mark. She said she could be open and affectionate and nothing would be misinterpreted. I kind of think that's why she was so easy to talk to for me."

"How do you know she's gay? They don't wear signs." Eddie got up and poured more coffee. "Or purple or rainbow stuff like on her car or something."

"Of course not. That's dumb, Eddie. There's just clues, that's all.

"I remember there used to be a thing about earrings with gay guys. It was supposed to be some sort of signal depending where you wore an earring, if you wore it in your left or in your right ear. But I never could remember which ear."

"Now a lot of gay people have wedding rings so you never know," I said, "besides, who cares anyway."

"Right. But why did you think she was gay?"

"Well, I guess because she had on a sweatshirt for the Thorns—"

"A lot of people like women's soccer. And women's basketball, too, and all women's sports—not just gay women."

"I know that. If you'd shut up and let me finish—it wasn't just the sweatshirt. She has that look—short hair, athletic, no make-up and was going to travel with her woman, friend." I said, holding up my fingers and putting air quotes around "friend."

"Oh well, maybe. But the main thing is that you were friendly and welcoming." Eddie leaned back and crossed his arms. "Listen, George, I got a good sense of how Lottie operates and we gotta get better stuff."

"What d'ya mean, better stuff?"

"Her beach house is really classy. She has a nice plush rug in front of the pull-out couch, and near the head of the bed there are throw pillows in pretty colors and a fancy comforter is folded at the foot. Compared to her place, ours looks pretty shabby."

"I think the things we got at Target are perfectly good. Besides, we haven't made any money and I don't intend to spend one more dime until we see if this business is going to get off the ground." I took my cup to the sink. "I'm tired, Eddie. All this socializing is getting to me. I'm going to take a nap."

I was exhausted. For the past two years, except mornings when Eddie came by for coffee, I'd had the house all to myself. I could be a complete slob and sit around and do nothing and no one would care. But since Eddie moved in—just a few short weeks ago, Lottie had been here (which was very tense because of what happened on the church field trip) and the O'Gradys had come (which was a total unmitigated disaster) and now Molly Gorman was here. Even though she was nice—it was all too much. Besides having to socialize with her, both last night and this morning—talking and trying to be friendly, there was the confusion of how I was supposed to act. Like having breakfast with her, and then her clearing the table like a thoughtful guest and not just a customer. I took off my shoes, fell into bed and stared at the ceiling.

I don't know if I can do this, Bess.

You're doing great, honey.

You used to get energized around people. Me—I'm just the opposite.

We were a good match. I pepped you up, and you slowed me down.

We never would have gotten together if Vince hadn't been killed.

You never know, George.

I was your friend, only that.

Your friendship was like gold.

It happened because he died, Bess.

And you were tender, and gentle.

How could I not have been?

No one had ever cherished me before.

I don't know why not. And I will forever.

I did cherish her. And I always had, long before that first time we made love, and luckily I'd had a little experience before Bess.

One of my professors in the College of Engineering at the U helped get me a summer job on a fishing boat in Alaska. It was grueling, difficult, dangerous work and whatever confidence I gained about being able to make my way in this world came from both the physical and the mental challenges I faced on the F/V Arctic Fox. Once we were out at sea there was no escape, so I had no choice but to learn to master my fear because the danger was constant and relentless. Getting washed overboard was a continuous threat, but the serious injuries from working the hydraulic machinery were far from uncommon. And I had to learn to get along with the crew who enjoyed making a fool out of a college kid. Being a hard worker, and not much of a talker was a big help and although I never became one of them, they came to good-naturedly tolerate me. When we'd come in to Ketchikan near Trident Seafoods there were women, none of them that young, who were ready to take care of us. Not experiences that would break your heart since money was involved, but a human connection for a lonely kid. So when Bess came to me that night I wasn't a virgin.

It was our senior year at the U. Her parents were away at a conference of some sort, I can't remember what it was, but I suppose it had something to do with the church. I was living in the dorm and they asked me if I'd housesit for them. They would be away for a little less than a week and I think they'd asked Bess first, but she had early morning classes and wasn't able to do it so they asked me. All I had to do was feed the cat, water the plants, and bring in the paper and the mail. I came over first thing in the morning for the cat, then stayed on campus the rest of the day and just went there at night when it was time to hit the hay.

The night before Rev. and Mrs. Braxton were supposed to get home, I hadn't been asleep for very long when I thought I heard something. I was a little groggy when I turned on the light and went downstairs. It was a nasty night and it could have been something the wind had caused. I don't remember what else I might have imagined or expected, but I know it wasn't Bess.

She clung to the banister at the bottom of the stairs as if she couldn't stand on her own. When she looked up tears were streaming down her face.

"Bess? What happened?" I rushed down to her and when I got to the bottom stair she reached for me and collapsed into my arms, sobbing. I sat on the step and held her. I only slept in shorts and her face and body were pressed against my bare chest and her tears were warm and wet against my skin. After a while the sobs subsided as she tried to get her breath. She drew her head back and stared at me, unable to speak, then buried her face between my neck and shoulder.

I didn't know what to do so I stroked her hair and her back. Finally, she was able to get the words out.

"Vince is dead—"

"Oh, no ..."

"He was drunk and took a curve too fast and slammed into a tree."

"Oh, Bess—"

"I-I need to lie down."

I took her hand and then put an arm around her waist and helped her up the stairs to her old room. "Can I get you anything?"

She shook her head, dazed, as she flopped on the bed like her limbs were rags and I took off her shoes and helped her off with her jacket. She lay there with her eyes closed, breathing with labored gulps. After a few minutes, she struggled to prop herself up and pulled the covers down and got under them. I sat on the edge of the bed and stroked her forehead. When her breathing was steadier, I started to get up.

"Don't leave."

"But—"

"Stay with me." She pulled back the covers and moved over making room for me.

Although I wasn't able to grasp it at the time, it was years later I came to understand that there can be a powerful connection between death and sex—as if there's a human instinct to connect and merge in the face of death and loss. Maybe to affirm creation. To affirm life. But I knew what it was for Bess that night: an act of comfort in the most profound way possible. And I knew what it wasn't: that she would now love me in any way other than the deepest friendship.

We never talked about what happened, not until a couple of months later—when we had to.

I sometimes wondered if Vince had lived if she would have at some point been able to end it. As long as he was alive, she kept going back to him—I suppose he was like a drug for her, some powerful alchemy of sex, excitement, and danger that she couldn't bring herself to shake. I always wished I could have had that effect on her. And, typically, I wondered what it would have been like to have that kind of effect on any woman, to have some kind of amazing sexual charisma instead of being good ol' boring George.

FREE WILLY

THIS TIME THERE WAS ONLY ONE MOUSE. IT PROBABLY took it about one nanosecond to find the trap—the Velveeta must have made it think it had discovered an exquisite little restaurant with a mouse Michelin star. I just hoped it didn't have a lot of pals who could sniff Velveeta from a great distance, from miles and miles away, breathing in its rubbery cheesy essence through their little mouse nostrils and then, traveling together, form a big caravan destined for Bluebell Nook. I shut the basement door behind me and was carrying the trap up the path when I saw Molly drive up.

"Oh, it looks like you've got it," she said, as she got out of her car.

"By Jove!" I exclaimed and tipped an imaginary hat like Henry Higgins and then felt dumb. Extremely stupid. I don't know why, but something had rattled inside my head and got a screw loose. Henry Higgins? *Really?* When I got to the top of the path I hoped to quit sounding like a fool. I tried to regain my professional host persona and said, "I think this should do the trick and keep them away. The last time I caught a couple, I think I let them go too close to the house. This time I'm going to let it go in Island Center Forest—"

"Island Center Forest?"

"It's a big park in the middle of the island—it has over 400 acres of forests, meadows, a pond, wetlands and miles of trails. Supposedly there are over 70 different kinds of birds. I think it should be very happy there."

"Like some company?"

"Say again?"

"I wondered if you'd like some company."

"Company? To get rid of the mouse?" I didn't know what to say. It was the whole confusing thing again about how I was supposed to act. I knew I should try to be friendly to the guests, and I'd been doing my impersonation of a good host the best I could—but my truck was a grungy mess. It didn't seem appropriate to have a guest ride in a vehicle that hadn't been washed in months (years, actually). It wasn't that I would mind taking her with me, but my truck was embarrassing. I know I was hesitant, because she immediately explained, "No problem, if it doesn't work for you—it's just that I'd love to see more of the island." She had a such a warm, easy manner. Maybe the truck wouldn't bother her that much.

"Well, sure—I mean if you don't mind riding in my truck. It's kind of messy."

"I can hold the mouse."

"Okay."

"I just need to stop in the room for a minute," she said. "If you don't mind waiting."

"I'll wait here by the truck." I watched her jog down the path to the basement. She was quite spry, like a cute aging tomboy, and if my crappy truck didn't bother her and she wanted to help release the mouse and see more of the island—it was fine by me. Besides, maybe she missed her girlfriend and wanted company.

I quickly scooped up as much junk from the floor as I could: an oily rag, a sea of used paper coffee cups, a lot of old *Beachcombers*, a broken pair of sunglasses, a bunch of empty Frito bags. (Fritos are a superior snack. I think they are to chips, what Triscuits are to crackers.) She came back as I was taking the junk to the garbage can. It seemed pretty quick, she probably wasn't the type to spend a lot of time in front of the bathroom mirror like some do. I held the passenger door open and she thanked me as she climbed up into the truck, shoving some Frito bags to the floor that I hadn't gotten off the seat. She reached over for the trap. "Here, I'll take it." I handed it to her and she held it on her lap and smiled at the mouse stuck inside; I actually think she liked the little thing.

"I have to say, this place is really beautiful. I got a map of the island at the grocery store and went to see the lighthouse at Pt. Robinson. I couldn't have picked a more beautiful day."

"You could see Mt. Rainer then?"

She nodded. "Absolutely breathtaking."

"I never take it for granted, and I've lived here all my life."

"On the island?"

"Seattle. But we wanted a more rural place and it wasn't that expensive back then. And the commute to Boeing wasn't too bad."

"Was it Eddie's idea to start the Airbnb?"

"Yeah, he's a lot more social than I am."

She looked out the window as we bounced down the

drive to the road. She seemed oblivious to the layer of dust all over the dashboard and the junk that was still littering the floor. We drove north along Vashon Highway and when we came to Quartermaster Harbor, I had to slow down where the road sloped next to the water.

She reached over and patted my arm. "Thank you."

"Um, what for?"

"Slowing down next to the water so I can get a good look—it's just beautiful."

"Had to. It's 25 here and in Burton. Sometimes the Sheriff pops out and catches speeders."

She laughed. "Is there a place to pull over? I'd love to take a picture."

"I can pull over before we get to Burton."

"Burton? Is that another town on the island?"

"Not really. It's just a little grocery store and a post office. Oh, and a gas station, a marina, a flower stand and a couple of businesses. But not exactly a town."

I pulled over next to some steps that went down to the beach, and she took her phone out, put down the window, and snapped a picture. The water was calm, silvery like glass and you could see a few people in red and yellow kayaks near the Burton peninsula.

"Thanks." She put up the window, and looked at the photo she'd just taken. "I'm going to send this to Joan, and show her what she missed so she'll want to come next time."

"Too bad she couldn't make it—"

"I know, and she'd really love it here—she loves being near the water." She looked at the kayakers, then glanced at me. "Do you do much boating?"

"Eddie and I like to fish."

"Being retired must be great—with more time for fishing."

"We haven't done much lately."

"I guess the Airbnb takes up your time."

"Maybe." I didn't want to go into it. How I'd been stuck for two years. And Eddie, except for a couple of ventures (which were complete fiascos) for all his bravado, had been stuck living in the attic waiting for Marlene's father to die. What a miserable pair.

"Retirement can be tricky, I think. At least it has been for me. My husband and I ...

Her what? ... Husband ... A man? A husband is usually a man. I don't have much of a poker face and I was trying to look very casual and not at all surprised and confused, which is what I was. I hoped she was looking at the scenery and not at me. Who was the husband? What kind of a husband? These days there are men who used to be women, and vice-versa, and people who don't want to be called "he" or "she." You're supposed to call them "they"—Eddie's niece wants to be called "they" and he had trouble remembering to do it. He found it very confusing and I would, too. I agreed with Eddie about that. I mean people can be called whatever they want, but it's hard to remember when it's a new way to say things. Bess's father always said he didn't care what people called him as long as they called him for dinner. He wasn't that much of a jokey person, but he said that one a lot. And Bess always gave him a little courtesy laugh. I wish I could have some advice right about now because everything just changed. It was as if it had been pleasant and calm and then the wind suddenly came up. That had happened to me and Eddie once when we were fishing near Fern Cove. We just got slammed. The wind came from nowhere and the boat got tossed around.

Up to a few minutes ago, I had been pretty comfortable with Molly, maybe "comfortable" was too strong a word. Maybe just a couple of degrees less tense than I usually am with people I don't know. If there was a scale between totally terrified and blissed out, I had landed around in the middle with Molly. But now I was heading back down the scale, passing awkward and hovering toward nervous. Talk about stuck—I couldn't think of a thing to say, and just stared straight ahead as I drove along Vashon Highway toward 188th where one of the trailheads to the forest is located. There are four trailheads into the forest, but I liked this one because it's close to Meadowlake Pond and there's a nice bench where you can sit and listen to the frogs. I tried to think about frogs. Nature is very calming.

Molly continued talking but her words were fuzzy. They just hung around in the air like you were listening to someone on a cell phone where the connection breaks up and maybe you'd get a word or two, but you couldn't understand what was being said. Even though I thought about frogs, I was stuck on *husband*. I couldn't tune in to anything else she was saying. I clammed up. Or turtled up because I was more like a turtle venturing out that got poked and put its head back in the shell. And I was still blank, no words came to my foggy brain. Her husband? Well, I guess I got that one wrong. I tried to look relaxed, but I noticed I was drumming my fingers on the steering wheel, fast skittery tapping, like little mini jackhammers. I stopped it, but as we passed the Vashon Art Center I noticed it had started up again, like my fingers had a mind of their own.

As I turned left on 188th she peered over at me, like she expected me to say something.

I just glanced at her like I was clueless. Which I was.

She must have thought the reason I looked confused was because I didn't hear too well. So she leaned toward me and spoke quite loud, enunciating each word. "It's funny how that happens sometimes, don't you think?"

"Um, I don't know," I mumbled.

"Well, that's how it turned out," she continued, still talking loud. "We had a small construction business. I was the office manager and after Dennis died, I kept working and it was a salvation really. We were swamped with work and it helped me focus and just keep going. We'd applied for a state grant to provide apprenticeships and training for felons, ex-offenders, and the grant came through three months before he died, so even though I was overwhelmed with getting the program going—it was the best thing that could have happened."

My fingers kept tapping on the steering wheel. The husband she had was dead. Joan was her pal, her girlfriend. Dennis was the husband. I kept trying to digest these facts.

Tell her about me, George.

What am I supposed to say?

Tell her you had a wife and I died.

That's kind of personal.

She told you about her husband.

That doesn't mean I have to tell my stuff.

George, am I stuff?

That's not what I meant. Stuff about my life. You were my whole life, Bess.

And you have to carve out a new life now. Talk to her.

I dunno if I can.

It wasn't so hard to talk with her when she was gay.

She was never gay.

Go ahead, just think of it as practice.

What should I say?

I waited for Bess to put some suggestions in my head, but there was nothing and all I could hear was the springs of the truck and the gravel crunching as I drove into the parking lot. Molly looked down at the mouse. She seemed sad.

"I'm sorry about your husband," I said quietly.

She looked over at me and nodded. "Thank you." Then she just sat there looking at the trapped mouse on her lap.

I got out of the truck and went around to the passenger side and opened the door. She handed me the trap and then climbed down. We walked next to each other across the gravel to the wide trail at the edge of the forest.

"It was two years ago, and sometimes it seems like yesterday and then there are days that it seems like it was a long time ago. That's strange, isn't it?"

I didn't say anything. And she stepped closer to me and asked if I had trouble hearing her sometimes.

"No, I hear okay. It's just that it's the same for me."

"What is?"

"That it was two years ago that Bess died, but sometimes is seems like yesterday and then sometimes it seems like many years."

"Bess?"

"My wife."

She looked puzzled, and stood there like she didn't know what to say. "Oh, I thought—well, you know I just assumed ..." Her face was flushed.

I knew right away what she thought and surprised myself because without even a prompt from Bess, I just came right out and told her. "Eddie's my friend. He and his wife Marlene are getting a divorce. He needed a place to crash."

She nodded like she was trying to get her head around it.

"It was his idea for us to do this Airbnb thing. I don't know how long he's going to stay at my place. But I wanted to help him out."

She stopped in front of the big map that showed all the trails. She stared at the map and shuffled the gravel with her toe. I didn't know what else to say and the silence got awkward. I felt slightly better after I explained about me and Eddie, but silence is always uncomfortable for me and now the feeling spiked. It was up a notch (or at least two or three) and instead of trying to think of something else I could say to her, I looked at the mouse. His life must have felt extremely strange and scary, being stuck in the trap like that. It helps me to think of a situation that is worse off than mine.

After a while, she sighed. "You and Eddie. That's how we get by, isn't it?" Then she looked up at me. "The Beatles got it right—we get by with a little help from our friends."

Help from our friends—that made me picture having tea with Martha Jane and our talks in her cozy kitchen and I guess it loosened me up because the awkward feeling went down a few notches and I said, "Bess's dear friend lives down the hill at Baker's Beach. And I hang out with her a lot. Well, not just Bess's friend—she's my friend, too. And I have to say she's helping me get by."

"Joan's like that. She's the kind of friend that if I needed to, I could call her at 3:00 in the morning. Not that I would. But I could. And I'm there for her like that, too."

"Well, maybe this guy will find a friend in the forest." I pointed to the map. "You can walk for miles in here, it's huge."

"And they allow dogs," she said, noticing the stand with a dispenser of poop bags and the sign that said people had to leash their dogs and pick up the poop. "Aggie would love it here. I saw on your website that you allow dogs and I kind of wish I'd brought her. But Shannon, my granddaughter, loves Aggie, so I usually leave her with my stepson's family when I travel. Both he and my daughter-in-law are at work all day, and Shannon's at school. They don't think it's fair to leave a dog alone all day, so they don't have one. But they love Aggie."

"What kind of a dog?"

"She's a rescue. Part Golden Retriever and something else, but she mostly looks like a Golden Retriever. Aggie's a great dog." She seemed to realize that she'd been talking fast. Then she said, "Maybe we better let the mouse go."

"Okay." I pointed to the map. "If we take the main trail, and then this one that goes off to the right, we'll come to a nice pond. There's a bench there and it might be a good place to let him go."

"Or her."

"Right. Whatever it is. We can let it go and if you want, we can sit and watch it leave the trap."

"Like *Free Willy*." She laughed. "That was my stepson's favorite movie."

The wide trail wound through a forest thick with tall, second growth fir and cedars. At the base of the trees, large ferns with lush fronds spread out in great, abundant arcs like they belonged in an ancient rain forest. The evergreen smell was dense and fresh and, along with the deep earthiness, made me feel both invigorated—and at the same time, more relaxed. It also made me realize I should have gotten out more like this the past couple of years, instead of staying stuck in my house. Nature takes you out of yourself; it can make your troubles seem smaller. And on the island it's

not like a city where you have to be in a park with tons
of other people, or drive for hours to experience it. It's
easy to be in the forest, or on beaches, or in so many
places where you can see the mountains. Almost everywhere it's green and quiet and beautiful. Like gold in
my backyard that I'd been too miserable to even notice.

The sunlight made lacey lemony patterns through
the branches and the forest was a kaleidoscope of green.
I carried the trap and we walked side by side along the
trail. We didn't say anything, and as we walked farther
into the forest I realized the silence was starting to be
okay. It didn't bother me much. Molly was looking all
around and taking deep breaths like she was trying
to drink in the forest. Then she stopped and bent her
head back, staring straight up into the trees.

"What's that sound?"

"Ravens."

"Really? It sounds like monkeys howling."

"They make a lot of different sounds. Sometimes
it's a low gurgling croak, or these harsh grating sounds,
or a shrill alarm call. Their sound is a lot deeper than a
crow's and you can hear it for over a mile, it's so loud.
And it really echoes in here." I was far from being any
kind of field guide authority, but it made me happy to
be able to tell her about the ravens.

"It almost sounds like a jungle filled with monkeys."

"I never thought of that. But you're right." I looked
down at the trap. "The trail I told you about is up here
just around the bend. When we get to the pond we can
let it out."

After we had walked for about ten minutes we
passed a man and woman who looked about my age,

seventy-something, although it's really hard to tell about age. They were walking their dog, a big, black Lab.

"Great day," the guy said.

"For sure." Molly smiled, as we passed them. When they were out of sight, she said, "They were the first people we've seen. I'm surprised there haven't been more."

"The forest covers four hundred acres and it just absorbs a lot of people."

It took us another ten minutes to get to the pond and when we got to the edge of it, Molly stopped. "What a gem!"

"Do you want to sit on the bench?"

"Sure."

I sat next to her holding the trap. "I was thinking I could put it out near the weeds."

"That would be good."

"Bess liked it too."

"Liked what?"

"That movie. About the orca getting free. She liked a lot of those kid type movies where they didn't have a lot of violence. *Anne of Green Gables*, that sort of thing."

"I feel the same way about violence, I don't want to watch it. It's disturbing and awful. And I can't stand how it seems commonplace. And they just make things more and more gory—I think it's sick." And then after a minute she added, "Although I do like a good mystery—not a thriller, but *Miss Marple* or *Poirot*—or anything that's like Agatha Christie's cozy mysteries."

"Those are very nice."

Bess didn't like the violence, but she didn't mind movies with sex. But I kept the thought about sex to myself. And then I wondered—would I have mentioned sex in movies if Molly was gay? Who knows? Very confusing.

I walked over to the edge of the pond and knelt down, put the trap next to the weeds and opened it. Then, nothing. The mouse just stayed there.

"So much for Free Willy." I went back to the bench and sat next to Molly again.

"Maybe it likes it in there. The way some dogs seem to feel safe in a crate."

"Maybe it's elderly, and has dementia. Mice only live about a year, or a year and a half. So this could be its twilight years." I looked at the trap and it was still sitting in there.

"Getting old is hard." Molly said, as she looked out at the pond.

"You can say that again."

"Okay. Getting old is hard." Molly laughed.

That made me laugh.

"What can we do but laugh?" She looked over at me. "I mean, it's all downhill so we might as well enjoy the ride."

"I agree, but it's harder for some folks."

"I had a health scare recently—but everything's okay. But it just gets your attention, you know. You begin to re-evaluate everything. At least I did."

"A wake-up call."

She nodded. "Although just being in your seventies is a wake-up call, if you know what I mean. And then when you lose your husband, or your wife. Well, you know what it's like … I don't have to tell you."

"My friend Martha Jane found a dead guy on her beach. And nobody knows who it is, who he was. She tried to find out, but there's no information and I guess there are a lot of people like that. They just die and no one knows anything about them. I have to say it shook me up." I wasn't sure I wanted to explain why that guy bothered me so much, but I didn't need to decide because just then she jumped up and pointed to the trap.

"Look! It's gone!" She turned to me, held up her hand and we high-fived.

We stayed by the pond for a while after the mouse left and Molly told me more about herself. She'd gone to college at the University of Oregon and had been engaged to a guy who ended up getting killed in Vietnam.

His father was a Marine, and unlike a lot of students at Oregon who were against the war and were in anti-war protests, her fiancé felt serving was his duty. "He actually signed up. He was in the 1st Marine Division and was killed in September of 1967 in a search and destroy mission in the Que Son Valley." Then she became quiet for a while—finally she sighed and said, "Over fifty thousand killed." She shook her head. "What a waste. *What a complete waste.*"

"I was lucky, I never got drafted." That was all I wanted to say about it.

"You were lucky."

"You can say that again."

She smiled. "I won't this time."

Then she went on to tell me more about herself and it was comfortable because I didn't feel like I had to say much. It was nice just listening. She told me at Oregon she had gotten a degree in accounting. She liked math and most small companies always needed someone and it was usually easy to find work. "That's what I did at my husband's business, that and generally manage the office. It worked out pretty well, for the most part. Dennis had been married and divorced and had a five-year old son when we got together. There wasn't much joint custody back then, so we just had Tommy on the weekends."

"So you're a stepmother—I guess you had mentioned him. They have your dog."

"Right. And a granddaughter, although she's actually a step-granddaughter. We didn't have our own kids. Dennis didn't want any more." Molly didn't say anything for a while. She just sat on the bench very still, staring at the pond in silence.

The subject of kids wasn't easy for me and I looked at the weeds hoping to see a frog.

Finally, she said, "Dennis called all the shots in our marriage—and I let him."

I didn't know what to say.

"I wonder sometimes … do you think people can change?"

"I hope so. But sometimes I think that even though I'm an old man, inside there's a thirteen-year old kid that got stuck."

She laughed. "I can relate to that. My whole life I've tried to please people. Just like I did when I was in junior high. And honestly, for decades it hasn't been that different. I wanted people to like me. Even people I *didn't* like—I wanted to like me. And when you want that too much, you put up with a lot of things you shouldn't. But I'm trying to change. Since Dennis died it's the first time in my life I can make decisions just for me. I'm trying to figure out what I want, and believe me, it's a new experience."

"I heard on the radio that the neurons in our brains can still make new connections at any age, so maybe people can learn to be different in some ways."

"That would be nice. I hope my neurons can do that." She looked over at me. "Do you have kids."

"No. We just had each other."

"I admit not having that responsibility has its advantages. People who don't have kids certainly have freedom. Even though I have my stepson and his family, we've never been that close. I do help out when they need me and they take Aggie when I travel, but that's about it. I've been thinking about my relationship with them—it's another part of my life I'm trying to evaluate.

"When I look back, ever since he was five, I think Tommy felt disloyal to his mother whenever he was with me and Dennis. And since Dennis died, he and his wife haven't once asked me to dinner. I used to give Tommy a gift every year on his birthday, but he never thanked me. He's on Facebook all the time, posting things about sports teams—so he has plenty of time for that, but can't find the time to send even a text or email of thanks. So I quit. Maybe that's petty, I don't know. It didn't bother me so much when Dennis was alive, or not enough to stop sending a gift. But now I don't want to bother. Sometimes I wonder if I'm holding a grudge, but when I see all his Facebook stuff I don't care if I am." Molly sighed, "And they're not even teaching Shannon how important it is to acknowledge a gift, which really annoys me because it's not doing her any favors." She paused and shook her head. "Oh my, how'd I get started on that?"

"Kids. And not being close to them."

"Right. Well, I've accepted it—I think. Although I guess not completely, or I wouldn't have gone on about it. But I am learning to enjoy my independence. I suppose the only thing that lurks in the back of my mind is the worry that I might fall down and conk out and no one would know."

"I sure understand that worry."

"I can't believe I've said all this," she smiled, shaking her head again. "I suppose it's like being up above the clouds on a plane, and you sit next to a stranger, and you get to talking and tell the person all kinds of things because you're totally detached from your life, and you'll never see the person again."

I didn't know how to take that, so I just stared at the pond, hoping to see some frogs.

BESS

MOLLY WANTED TO GET HOME BEFORE PORTLAND'S rush hour, and after she checked the ferry schedule she decided to try for the 12:10 boat that goes from Tahlequah to Pt. Defiance in Tacoma. The minute we pulled up to the house, she flung open her seatbelt, jumped out of the truck, ran down to the basement room, grabbed her stuff, charged back to her car, threw in her bag, said a hurried good-bye and left. Ferries can make people who don't live here nervous. People living here have accepted the fact that, as Bess often said, "our lives are ruled by the ferry gods." Otherwise they'd be a wreck. Missing a boat can be a fact of life. But it's different for visitors. I just wished she'd said something more than that quick good-bye.

After she left, I sat at the kitchen table trying to decide what to do with myself. The next guest was a lady from Seattle; she was coming alone and had booked for two nights. Eddie had taken the call and evidently she loved Scotland, so he arranged for Scottie to be here tonight. There was plenty to do to get ready for her: clean the room, strip and wash the sheets, make up the bed, put up fresh towels and soap, set the smart mouse trap, go to Thriftway to get more wine—but I just sat there. Like a blob. I couldn't get motivated. Besides, I wasn't going to do it without Eddie—that was for sure! And this morning he said he wouldn't be back until around 1:00. The house was quiet. Not a calm and contented quiet; but something lifeless and empty and as I sat in the plaid chair, my mind went to what Molly had said about her marriage. About her husband calling all the shots. It didn't sound like a marriage made in heaven. But I suppose there are people who just go along and make it work even though it wasn't the stuff of their dreams.

Bess was my dream. From high school on, she was everything I'd ever hoped for—ever dreamed of—it never once wavered for me. Not once. But I had no illusion that the night Vince died and we made love, that for her it reflected anything more than the deepest friendship with her heartbreaking need for comfort and human connection. But there was a change in our relationship after that night—she wanted to see more of me. We met most evenings in the library where we'd sit across from each other and study. Bess didn't want to talk, but it was clear she had a need to be with me. I could have been a service dog, the way I sat at her side, providing quiet support and companionship. And I didn't mind the role. "For Once in My Life" was my theme song that year. Stevie Wonder could have written it about me. "For once in my life, I have someone who needs me. Someone I've needed so long."

Sometimes we'd go to the movies. It was a night in May, a month after Vince had been killed, when she wanted to talk. We were coming back from seeing

Midnight Cowboy and ended up in one of the taverns on the Ave, the main drag next to the university.

"Pretty depressing," she said, as she sat down. We were in a booth toward the back where it was quieter. "What a sad movie."

"Yeah, pretty sad," I nodded. "But in the end it was about love, at least that's what I got out of it."

"What a strange pair. I guess people have a way of finding each other. Or who they need."

She was quiet for a long time. She'd ordered a coke but hadn't touched it. Then she excused herself and went to the restroom. When she came back, she didn't say anything. She seemed upset, and it made me wish we'd gone to a more upbeat movie. *Sweet Charity* was playing, a musical with Shirley MacLaine based on a Broadway show by Neil Simon. We both had seen a couple of movies he wrote, *Odd Couple* and *Barefoot in the Park*, and thought they were great. His stuff was always good for a laugh, and I was trying to remember whose idea it was to go to such a sad movie.

Bess leaned forward as if she were gathering her nerve. Her voice caught in her throat and she looked down for minute and then directly at me.

"I'm pregnant, George."

"Oh …" That was all that came out of my mouth, just *oh*.

"You're …"

"I'm sure. I've been to the clinic."

"Oh, well, I mean …"

"I'm almost three months."

"So, not from the night we …" It was the first time either of us had mentioned that we'd made love.

"It would be easier if it was."

"Vince's?" What a stupid thing to say. If it wasn't mine, of course it was Vince. I didn't mean to imply that she slept around. *Jesus.*

She nodded.

So I just nodded and we didn't say anything for a while.

Finally, she said, "There aren't too many choices. I have a friend who knows a doctor—"

"Abortion?"

She nodded.

"That can be dangerous."

"Someone else I know went to Japan. It's legal there," she sighed. "But I don't know how I'd pull that off. It would be complicated."

I felt so bad for her. Her hands were folded on the table as if she were trying to hold herself together. I reached over and took her hand. Her eyes filled with tears.

"Let's get married." I don't know why it took me so long to figure out the solution, because it was so obvious.

"George …" She took her hand away and wiped her eyes. "I could have the baby and put it up for adoption."

"Is that what you want?"

"I don't want you to do this because you feel sorry for me. Or be a hero."

"I love you, Bess."

She nodded, and I took her hand again.

"More than a friend," I said. "I mean, we are friends, but I'm in love with you and have been for a long time."

"It wouldn't seem fair." She shook her head. "You know you mean the world to me—but I … I care about you and I—"

"Look, Bess. I know you see me as a friend—I wouldn't expect you to feel anything else. But I want to marry you—be with you—and your caring for me is enough, I'll take it. I'll take you on any terms ... I want you. And I'm sure I can be a better father than my dad was."

She sat very still and just looked down, then wiped her eyes.

"I want to, Bess. I mean it. Just think about it."

I never questioned wanting to marry her. I loved her. That was all there was to it. Although I have to admit I did question how I'd feel about the baby. If it turned out to be a boy who looked like Vince, would Bess only have eyes for him? Would I just become part of the furniture? Could I love him, even though being Vince's son wasn't his fault? But those fears were mainly in the background because the strongest feeling I had was an intense need to protect Bess. I don't think it's an innate male thing, but I'd had practice. It was the role I took on from a young age with the most important woman in my life, my mother. After my father left, she seemed fragile to me. She was withdrawn and very tired much of the time; and I learned to pull my own oar and as much of hers as I could. And after she got sick, the need to take care of her just increased. I remember Bess's father telling me I'd done a good job at being the man of the house.

But as much as I thought I was protecting Bess, it was Bess who protected me. From loneliness. And she eased my insecurity. Without a father, and not wanting to be like the one I had; I assumed the persona of what I thought a man should be like. I made it up. *To Kill a Mockingbird* came out when I was in junior high and Atticus Finch was my idea of how to be a man: to be strong and brave and kind. Maybe I was kind, but when I attempted to acquire his other attributes, to be strong and brave—it was as phony as a cover song by a crappy garage band—because I didn't feel strong and brave. Weak and fearful was more like it. I knew my invented self was artificial and fraudulent, and that knowledge gave way to a type of social anxiety: the fear that I'd be found out. Luckily, fear wasn't operative at work; engineering was an area where I felt capable and I could focus well on a task. But I never aspired to management because I knew that in the role of a leader, having to evaluate and motivate people, and risk their criticism, my anxiety would get in the way.

I had worked the past two summers at Boeing and they offered me a job which would start right after I graduated in June. I was in the Class of 1969. It was a tumultuous year. The largest antiwar protest, the Vietnam Moratorium, brought over a half million people to DC in November, and in Seattle 3000 protested downtown at the courthouse and then at the Federal Office Building. Four years earlier, in 1965, both the college deferment from the draft and the exemption of married men ended, so in 1969 I could have been drafted in the lottery. But I did have a few things in my favor: Boeing was deemed necessary for the war effort and if that didn't work, Bess's father, Rev. Braxton, even though he wasn't part of one of the historically pacifist religions, Quaker, Mennonite, or

Church of the Brethen, he was willing to give it a try and attest to my conscientious objector status. It would have been a last ditch effort, but he would have been supported by his congregation. The church was located near the university and had a lot of liberal members. Many were professors who, along with their families, not only had supported civil rights throughout the sixties, but were strongly against the war. The people who rejected the liberal culture of the church had long gone, so offering to help me get out of Vietnam wouldn't have been a stretch for him. But luck—and the Grace of God, as Rev. Braxton said—was on my side and my number never came up.

Abortion wasn't a legal option in 1969. It would be another year before Washington became the first state to legalize abortion by a vote of the people in a referendum. At first Bess tried to hide her pregnancy while she figured out what she wanted to do. It wasn't that hard to hide, because long granny dresses—an earthy, hippie look, were common on campus.

But it wasn't long before her mother figured it out and because Bess and I had been spending so much time together, her parents assumed I was the father. And Bess didn't correct them. Rev. and Mrs. Braxton just expected we'd get married, which probably paved the way for Bess to go ahead with it. It never seemed like a clear, deliberate decision; but something which just vaguely evolved after her parents found out. It was as if she was a passenger on a train that had left the station and her father was the conductor. Her mother, even though she went along with it, wasn't too happy with the whole situation. Although she always followed

her husband's lead, deep down she was more traditional and she fussed and worried what people would
think when the baby came too soon after a wedding.
She was afraid it would reflect badly on her. But Rev.
Braxton genuinely supported our marriage. The world
seemed to be coming apart; the year before, in 1968
Martin Luther King, Jr. and Bobby Kennedy had been
killed, cities were burning and students were protesting
all over the world. The fact that we had to get married seemed minor to him. I think he just wanted Bess
to get through the late sixties unscathed and settled
down with a husband who had a steady job. It was also
typical in families like theirs for girls to marry right
after college. And her parents liked me. They saw me as
reliable, stable and decent. Rev. Braxton even took me
aside to say he thought I was a good influence on Bess.

We were married in June right after graduation. Rev.
Braxton married us in the small chapel off of the main
chapel in his church and Bess's mother was the only witness. The lawyer who handled my mother's estate helped
find a good realtor and advised me in purchasing a house
with the money that had come from the sale of my mother's house. The one we bought was a small boxy home
with turquoise aluminum siding near Northgate shopping mall. In those days the traffic had yet to become
terrible and the commute to Boeing was manageable.
We lived with Bess's parents until the sale closed, and I
started work at Boeing right after graduation.

In early July, a week after we moved out of the Braxton's
house, Bess had a miscarriage. It was an awful time. She

never said so, but I was sure on some level it was a relief for her. And when I could admit it, for me as well, because I no longer had to worry about being a father to someone else's child. But losing the baby brought another reality: Bess now had no reason to stay with me. I knew she was too honorable to suggest ending the marriage, so I did it for her. I had always heard about quickie divorces in Las Vegas, and I went to the library to see what information I could find. About three weeks after her miscarriage, I told her what I'd learned. Nevada only required a short residency and we could get a divorce there without too much fuss—and she could get on with her life.

But she didn't want any part of it. She was adamant. Unmovable.

And we stayed together for almost fifty years ... 'til death do us part.

I've thought a lot over the years why she made that decision. In spite of her wild child years with Vince, underneath she was pure goodness and so maybe she took our wedding vows seriously, or couldn't bear to hurt me—or her father, who had been so great about her pregnancy and our marriage. And in her way, I understood she cared for me. Today, all these years later, I knew she thought it was ridiculous that I was thinking about this old history. Sitting around in the plaid chair, reliving it when I should have been thinking about getting ready for the next guest at Bluebell Nook.

What's the point, George?

I don't know. I just wondered again.

It's water under the bridge, or over the dam. Whatever. I loved you.

I would have gone to Nevada. Made it easy for you.

You forget how depressed I was.

But you got out of it.

You were a life raft. Holding me every night the way you did.

But after you felt better, I didn't want you to feel like you had to stay.

I didn't feel like I had to. I needed you. I might not have made it without you, George.

You would have.

I'm not sure about that. But what does it matter? Why dredge this up now? Is it Molly?

Molly?

I know whenever you feel insecure, it triggers something and you wonder again.

I never talked about it.

But I knew. Molly, isn't it?

I hardly know her.

So get to know her.

She left in a rush.

So what. Get to know the next one.

You're going to say something about fish in the sea. I can hear you.

You're right. Of course I am. Now go.

NEXT GUEST

THE AFTERNOON AFTER MOLLY LEFT I WENT DOWN TO Martha Jane's house for tea. She was really excited—she'd been out on her deck painting that morning, and saw some orcas close to the shore. There are three groups of the whales that are in the Northeastern Pacific coastal waters and the southern residents are the ones we usually see, often near Point Robinson. But sometimes they're seen near Point Defiance in Tacoma, which is diagonally across from Baker's Beach.

"Oh, George," Martha Jane grinned, "I wished you'd been here—they were magnificent."

"I wished I had, too." Especially since after Molly left I was just sitting around like a snail stuck on a rock.

"Several of them breached!"

"Could you see how many?"

"It was hard to tell, maybe at least five. But how lucky could I be? If it hadn't been such a beautiful morning, I would probably have been inside reading and missed the whole show."

"There's a lot of luck in this world, that's for sure."

I had been lucky to be married to Bess, and maybe that was enough for one lifetime. Maybe when luck was handed out, it was decided that ol' George would get to have Bess and that would be his quota. I wished I could be more like Martha Jane. She'd had several husbands and she'd gone on to create a wonderful life on her own. I knew her well enough now to know that she was very sad about the losses in her life, but she had a spirit, some ability to find joy in simple things that fed her. Like her painting. And hanging out with her friends. And her cat. I wonder if you're just born with that.

"George, this morning when I saw the orcas, it got me thinking about Woody."

It always took me a minute to remember that was the dead guy.

"And then I thought about how the orcas meant so much to the Northwest Coast native tribes. The Tlingit viewed the orcas as a special protector, and Kwakiutl tribes believed that the souls of marine hunters turned into orcas upon their death. I don't like to call them killer whales, you know. Orca is a lovely name. I mean, I know they kill seals and other mammals to eat, but just think about Burger King and McDonald's and all the things people kill to eat. And we're called homo sapiens, human beings—not killer humans. So calling them killer whales doesn't seem fair to me."

"Orca does sound better," I agreed.

"Now what was I talking about George?"

"About Woody?"

"Oh, right. Thanks. Yes. So when I saw the orcas this morning and remembered about how some tribes believe the souls of some humans turned into orcas, it made me think about poor Woody and his soul. The Northwest Coast tribes have these rituals and I think if we don't hear something pretty soon about who he is, we should just go ahead and have a ritual for him."

"A funeral, or memorial service?"

"Exactly. We could think of it as helping his soul become some other form. And since he came to us from the sea, I think it might make sense to think of his soul turning into something fine and revered. Maybe like an orca, since he obviously didn't have that in this life."

It had occurred to me that Woody might not have been such a great guy in this life. But I thought it best not to go there. Martha Jane suggested we should both think about how we might conduct his memorial and talk again about our ideas of what it should be like.

I didn't have many ideas about that sort of thing, unlike Martha Jane who was very inventive. A lot of teachers have to be creative to keep students engaged, and I was sure having been one, she'd come up with something nice for Woody. He was lucky to have been found by Martha Jane, and not someone who didn't care that he had washed up on the beach like so much rubbish.

That night the next guest was to arrive—a woman named Carolyn Stein. (The next fish in the sea, according to Bess.) When she'd made the reservation she said in her email that she'd been attracted to our Scottish theme. Eddie printed out the email and waved it around, his finger punching the paper. "See George, having a theme was important! We beat the competition—we were just what she was looking for. No other Airbnb on the island has a theme like ours!"

When Eddie told Scottie we especially needed him

because the guest was interested in Scotland, he was over the moon. Her email said she'd be taking the 7:35 boat from Seattle. If there was no screw up with the ferry, we figured she'd arrive at Bluebell Nook around 8:15. Scottie got here almost forty-five minutes early. His outfit was all clean and pressed—even his cap with the ribbons in the back looked sharp, and he took his place in front of the fireplace and practiced his songs.

As soon as he heard a car, Scottie charged to the front door and flung it open. "Welcome to Bluebell Nook!"

"Oh my, don't you look wonderful!" She was taking a small bag from her car and Scottie, his kilt flapping, ran to carry it for her.

"It's okay, I've got it." She smiled, as she closed the car door.

"Let me. I insist. I can be the wind beneath your wings." As soon as he said that, she let out a big roar of a laugh and handed over her bag.

Eddie and I stood in the doorway and we both shrugged. No clue what that was about. But when they got to the door, Carolyn Stein looked so much like Bette Midler, she could have been her sister. Eddie and I both introduced ourselves and Scottie volunteered to take her to the room.

She smiled at Scottie. "Great, thanks—and then I'd love to hear you sing."

Scottie didn't need to walk her down to the basement room, he could have floated. Eddie and I went to the kitchen and brought out wine, grapes, Triscuits (on a plate—not just the box) and nice cheddar cheese. We were getting the hang of it and Carolyn Stein seemed to be such a cheerful person, we were off to a good start. When Scottie and Carolyn Stein came back, he walked in the door singing.

> *"O ye'll take the high road, and I'll take the low road.*
> *And I'll be in Scotland a' fore ye,*
> *But me and my true love will never meet again,*
> *On the bonnie bonnie banks o' Loch Lomond."*

Carolyn clapped, Scottie beamed, and Eddie and I thought we were probably just in the way because the two of them were really hitting it off. Then he sang two more songs,

"Annie Laurie" followed by "Will Ye Go Lassie Go" and after each song Carolyn clapped excitedly. After the last one, she even shouted, "Bravo!"

Eddie put his hand over his mouth and whispered, "hope he doesn't ask for more money."

I pretended I hadn't heard him.

Scottie held out his arms, about to belt out another one. "How 'bout 'Coming Through the Rye'?"

"Let's have 'Coming with the Wine' first, shall we?" Eddie pointed to the wine. "We have both red and white, which would you like, Carolyn ... Scottie? Or we have beer, too."

They both wanted red and I passed the plate of the Triscuits and cheese. "Oh, I forgot napkins." I went back to the kitchen for the napkins and Scottie asked Carolyn about her interest in Scotland.

"My daughter and her husband live there. My son-in-law teaches at the University of Edinburgh. He does stem cell research at the Scottish Centre for Regenerative Medicine there."

"It's one of the best universities in Europe." Scottie nodded, totally impressed.

"It is that," she said. "The place where he works, they grew a thymus grown from scratch inside an animal. It was a big deal—my son-in-law said they were the first to do that."

"What kind of an animal?" Eddie asked.

"I don't remember. I'm not too fond of animals. But they've had many Nobel Laureates there. But I can't remember their names." She took a sip of her wine. "I think there's something wrong with —"

"The wine?" Eddie sat forward.

"Oh no, the wine's very nice."

"I just mean that I think there's something wrong with the fact people know the names of the Kardashians, and I have no idea why, but no one can think of many Noble prize winners. And I'm as guilty of that as anyone, I'm afraid."

"But there are a lot of famous Scottish people that everyone does know about," Scottie said, proudly, "Charles Darwin, Robert Louis Stevenson, Sir Arthur Conan Doyle—to name a few."

"And J. M. Barrie. Everyone knows *Peter Pan*," she chimed in.

Bess always thought Wendy never got the credit she deserved in that story. Too much focus on the guy. And Tinker Bell because she was cute and little. I looked over at Scottie and Carolyn hitting it off and I was kind of fascinated how they seemed to be clicking so fast.

"... and Alexander Graham Bell, too," she added.

"I didn't know he was Scottish," Eddie picked up the bottle and held it over Carolyn's glass. "More wine?"

"Lovely. Thank you. Well, I didn't know he was from Scotland until I went over there. He immigrated of course, but not until he was through university. When he was in his twenties, he went to Canada first and then to Boston."

"Do you travel to Scotland with your husband?" Scottie asked. "And he couldn't come with you this weekend?"

He certainly got to it. Bess would be impressed— she'd wish I was more like Scottie. Bam. Right off the bat, he wants to know if she's available.

"We've been divorced for years. But he still sees our daughter, we just never go at the same time. But it's all very civil. Since I've been retired, I go as often as I can, but I had a hip replacement in April and my doctor thought it was best I wait a few more months before I travel. But I did want a little getaway here in the Northwest, and that's when I saw your website. The name certainly called to me, and then of course, I read you had a singer—"

"Call me Scottie," he piped up.

"Yes, I saw about Scottie and I was sold." She looked over at him. "Have you lived on the island a long time?"

"Not long—I'm divorced, too. And I've been a bit of a rolling stone, but I like it here and I hope to stay a while."

Scottie stared at her for a minute and didn't even blink. He made it obvious he was interested. She smiled at us and fluffed up her hair, then she yawned. "Well, guys—I think I better call it a night—we have tomorrow night, too," she said, smiling right at Scottie, "and I'll be ready for more music."

"Well, let's just have one for the road, the most famous song of Robert Burns," and then he sang.

"Should auld acquaintance be forgot,
And never brought to mind?
Should auld acquaintance be forgot,
And auld lang syne?"

Carolyn sang the chorus with him, both of them singing, *"For auld lang syne my jo, For auld lang syne …"*

She was no Bette Midler that was for sure, but she and Scottie sounded pretty good together, and then Eddie joined in and it was the three of them. *"We'll tak a cup of kindness yet, For auld lang syne."*

They held the last note for a while and then she jumped up, "Wonderful! Thank you!" and then she went over to Scottie and hugged him. "Great to be here—I'm looking forward to more tomorrow. Good-night, everyone." And she blew kisses to us and headed off to her room.

Scottie took his glass from the fireplace mantel and finished the last of his wine, then gathered up the other empty glasses and took them to the kitchen. It was the first time he'd been helpful like that. When he came back he grinned. "Well, George … Eddie …I'd say that went pretty well."

"You think?" Eddie slapped him on the back. "Great job, Scottie," he said, "see you tomorrow night!"

Scottie gave us thumbs up and a huge grin, and

headed out the door singing so loud I thought he could
be heard all the way down at Baker's Beach.

> *"Me and MY TRUE LOVE*
> *will never meet again ...*
> *... on the bonnie bonnie BANKS*
> *O' LOCH LOMOND!"*

CAROLYN

AFTER SCOTTIE LEFT, EDDIE SUGGESTED WE HAVE A nightcap to celebrate the success of the evening. He had a bottle of scotch that he kept in his room that he brought to the kitchen.

"How d'ya like yours?" Eddie asked. "I always take mine neat."

"Rocks with mine, thanks."

Eddie handed me my drink and then sat across from me. "Here's to a great evening." He raised his glass. "To Bluebell Nook."

"To Bluebell Nook." I raised my glass, clinked his, and then took a sip. It was good scotch, no wonder he hid it in his room.

We sat there quietly enjoying our drinks and I realized I was pretty surprised that Scottie had been such a big hit. Carolyn Stein had been so appreciative, so enthusiastic—she'd clearly had a great time.

"You know, George," Eddie finally said, "that couldn't have gone any better."

"I have to agree with you."

"You know what we did, George?"

"Provided a nice evening."

"Right. But it's what we *didn't* do," he said, proudly.

"What was that?"

"We didn't give up."

"After the mess with the O'Grady's."

"Right. After we had to give them a full refund and pay them not to write a bad review." Eddie sipped his drink, then set it on the table and made a tent of his hands, fingers touching each other. "A lot of weaker men might have thrown in the towel. But we stared failure right in the face and learned from our mistakes. They say you learn more from failure than success, and it's true. We also made a mistake on that Velveeta, and we tried again, we kept going—even when the Cheez Whiz nozzle got stuck."

"That was a mess, squirting all over everything."

"Yes, but we kept trying and we persevered." He picked up his drink and took a long swig.

"Carolyn did like the cheddar you got."

"We nailed it, George."

"And we moved on that mouse problem, right away," I added. "This afternoon I put six smart traps outside, spacing them evenly next to the foundation along the outer wall of the guest room—those little mice will be caught before they even think about going inside."

"Effective, on top of it—that's what we are. That's what it takes to run something well. Nip every problem in the bud and that's just what we did. We're a great team." Then Eddie stretched and yawned. "Well, I guess I'll turn in, buddy."

"Me, too. It's been a big day for us."

"Sure has. 'Nite, George."

"'Nite, Eddie."

Even though I was pretty tired, I didn't fall asleep right away. I was happy things had gone so well, but my thoughts kept jumping around. I started thinking about the way Scottie hit it off with Carolyn. He was on cloud nine. It was probably hard to be a septic guy when he'd really like to be able to support himself with music. I wondered what might happen with him and Carolyn tomorrow night. They sure seemed to have some chemistry. I'd say Scottie was smitten. Maybe she was, too, although it's hard to know since I'd just met her. But she didn't hold back at all, hugging him like that. I've never really known how to figure out women and their hugs. Never understood it. Sometimes, they're just a friendly thing, but then you don't know if they mean something else. How can you tell? Having these kind of thoughts seemed like the kind of thing a guy wondered about in junior high, which made me feel stupid. But there was no question that Carolyn really liked singing with Scottie and wanted to do more of it tomorrow night. There weren't any mixed signals there, it was very clear that she was interested in that. Not like Molly who just rushed off without a word. And said being so open with me was like being on a plane with a stranger you'd never see again. Did that mean she'd never see me again? She sure didn't say anything about coming back, although she mentioned she wanted to bring her friend. Or had she? Now I didn't trust my memory. But actions are what counts. And she hadn't called or emailed a word about coming back ... oh well, at least we knew Carolyn was up front about liking Bluebell Nook. And I was especially happy for Eddie.

So many of his money-making ideas hadn't panned out, in truth most all of them were failures.

I lay there looking at the ceiling thinking how quiet it was. Eddie usually starts snoring as soon as he hits the sack, but I hadn't heard anything and hadn't put in my earplugs yet. Then I heard a little tapping on the wall.

"George? You awake?"

"Yep." Sound carries in the drafty old house and I turned toward the wall between our rooms.

"Thanks for letting me crash here."

"Having a business wasn't such a bad idea."

"I think we're going to make it … I think I'm going to make it."

"Glad you're here, Eddie."

"Well, 'nite, George."

"Yep. Sleep well."

Not long after that Eddie began to snore, so I put in my earplugs and pretty soon I was out, too. I had a weird dream. It had people in it that I knew: Martha Jane, her neighbors Howie and Mark, Walter and Maggie Hathaway, and Albert and Bonnie Paugh and me. And it was a setting I knew well—Baker's Beach. We were having a memorial service for the dead guy and he was lying on the shore on a polished granite slab and we were grouped around it and Bette Midler was there and she was singing *Amazing Grace*. And then the dead guy, Woody, sat up and started singing. He sang the line … "that saved a wretch like me" … and then Bette Midler started screaming. She was screaming and screaming …

"George! What was that?" Eddie stood over me in his pajamas, shaking me. "You said you'd get all the mice!"

It was screaming all right—and it wasn't a dream—it had to be Carolyn. I sleep in my shorts so I quickly pulled on my pants and Eddie and I hurried to the living room. The screaming got louder and then there was pounding on the door and when Eddie opened it Carolyn burst into the room. She was in her nightgown and she was shaking and holding a bloody chicken. It looked dead.

"Oh my God!! Just look at this! Look at this!" she screamed. "There's BLOOD all over the place! WHAT'S OUT THERE!"

Eddie stood there in his pajamas staring at Carolyn. "It wasn't a mouse."

"What the hell are you talking about, you idiot! No mouse did this!"

I ran to the recycle pile and got a newspaper and took the chicken from Carolyn and wrapped it up. "I'm afraid it's dead."

"But it's head was moving!"

"They do that, but it's dead."

"Oh, my God!"

I set it on the kitchen counter and then got a rag and wiped up the blood that had dribbled all over the floor. I was on my hands and knees crawling around Carolyn while she stood there in her nightgown screaming at Eddie. There was blood on her nightgown, but, of course I couldn't blot it with little dabs or anything like that. I kept my head down and wiped the floor all around her and crawled over to the door and wiped up the blood that had dripped on her way in. It was good to have a focus. I was concentrating on the wiping, looking down at the floor, so Eddie got the brunt of everything.

"What happened?" Eddie mumbled, hiking up his pajama bottoms.

"*What happened?* There's a killer out there, you idiot! I heard some commotion and I went out to look. There was a big shadow—something running and then this!" She pointed to the kitchen counter where I'd put the chicken. "It flopped around and then it fell over! It was all bloody! What kind of a place is this? IT'S NOT SAFE HERE!" she shrieked.

I had finished wiping the floor, and I thought I'd better get up, although it took me a while, my knees are so creaky. I tried to calm her down, and give a reasonable explanation, "We do have coyotes and there have been cougars on the island but—"

"*What!* That's horrible!" She glared and me and Eddie, shaking so much that her nightgown was jiggling. Her face was very red. "I can't believe you want people to come here with wild animals all over the place."

Eddie held one hand on the waist of his pajama bottoms, which made me wonder if the elastic had given out. He tried to regain some composure. "I'm so sorry this happened. Can I get you a drink? Or some warm milk?"

"We're out of milk," I reminded him.

"Maybe a nice cup of tea. A cuppa as the Brits say," he said and smiled, trying to be charming.

"I don't want any tea!"

"It's herbal," Eddie said, "it might help your nerves."

"The only thing that will help my nerves is getting out of here! I'm leaving and I want my money back!"

Eddie and I just looked at each other. "Been there, done that," I muttered.

"We have to, George."

"I know. You're right."

I turned to Carolyn and tried to sound professional, and I think I was able to pull it off better than Eddie since I had on pants. "You'll get a full refund, Carolyn."

"I'm going to warn people about this."

Eddie and I looked at each other again and we nodded. Same song. Second Verse. A little bit louder and a little bit worse. "Would you take a little something not to write a review?" he asked.

"How little?"

"Fifty dollars?" Eddie suggested with a pleasant smile.

She just glared at us. "Not unless I get a full refund and eighty-five dollars. And I'm getting out of here right now! I don't care how late it is—I want off this terrible island!" she shrieked.

Carolyn stomped off, slamming the door so hard it shook and I went to the desk and got the Bluebell Nook checkbook. "Did she pay in advance?" I asked Eddie.

"She did. For both nights, so you have to write a check for $235."

I wrote the check, and then picked up the chicken I'd wrapped in the newspaper and went to take it out to the garbage. I stood at the door for a minute, listening for any creature that was still outside. But all I heard was an owl that was faraway and Carolyn in the basement room getting ready to leave. "Had to be a coyote, Eddie, unless there is another cougar on the island."

Eddie held his pajamas with one hand and raised his other arm making a fist like he was bound for battle. "I'm getting my gun!"

WOODY

I HAD A TERRIBLE SLEEP. ALL I COULD THINK ABOUT WAS Eddie and his gun and that he'd go out in the woods and shoot himself in the foot, literally, or (God forbid!) shoot some kid he mistook for the chicken-killer. What a nightmare! After hours of these horrible thoughts messing with my head, I was totally exhausted and finally did sleep. The next morning, I slept late and by the time I got up Eddie had gone, but there was a note by the coffee pot.

George—

I fed the chickens and there's coffee. I emailed the Nature Center first thing and they think there is another cougar on the island. Someone thought they spotted it down near Pt. Robinson. But I'm going to find that sucker and teach it a lesson it will never forget!

Remember, George—Carolyn Stein loved Bluebell Nook. It wasn't our fault her visit got ruined. So we can't give up now!!

WE have to be like Winston Churchill — NEVER, NEVER, NEVER GIVE UP!

Winston Churchill? *Really?* He's comparing one dead chicken to The Blitz! It was high time I put my foot down and end this whole Bluebell Nook fiasco. I would tell Eddie first thing when he got back that I was done, it was over—*fini*! I had to be firm. I wouldn't mince any words. This had gone on long enough.

But for all my resolve, no matter how determined I was and how hard I tried to pump myself up—I couldn't ignore the reality that for my entire life I have been the type that would prefer to avoid conflict whenever and wherever possible. Telling Eddie I was quitting would *not* be easy. He would not go gently into that good night away from our Airbnb. I didn't want to even imagine the unpleasantness of that conversation, and I was grateful that at least I had something to distract me. I had to leave to get to Baker's Beach by 2:00 pm. because Martha Jane had organized a memorial for Woody, the dead guy. She'd never been able to find out anything about him and decided to just go ahead with some sort of ritual. I wasn't exactly sure what she'd planned, but I hoped it would take my mind off the last night's shit show at Bluebell Nook.

It was unseasonably warm as I walked down to Baker's Beach. The blue sky shimmered and everything always felt brighter when I was going to be with Martha Jane. I could see the rhododendron in her front yard, its bright pink blossoms as big as basketballs. The day was gorgeous, and I was sure Martha Jane was happy that it was so beautiful for the memorial. She invited her neighbor Walter Hathaway and his wife, Maggie. Walter was an author of children's books and his wife Maggie was a retired librarian. They lived next to Baker's Beach and had just gotten back from the traveling they did each year. They put on programs and writing workshops for elementary school kids in rural parts of Washington and Oregon, and also on some Indian reservations. Walter played the ukulele and I'm sure he knew plenty of songs, although the only one in his repertoire I had ever heard him sing was "Won't You Come Home Bill Bailey." It was the way he called his dog whose name is Bill Bailey. He'd go out on his porch or on the beach with his ukulele and sing the song and then Bill Bailey always came home.

Martha Jane had asked Walter to play something for Woody's memorial. I had suggested *Amazing Grace*, but Martha Jane reminded me that we didn't know what religion Woody was and it would be better if this was a non-denominational service. She also invited her next door neighbors Howie and Mark. Howie had been a theatrical director and done some acting, too. He had an impressive voice that was deep and distinguished, like James Earl Jones' voice, and Martha Jane had asked him to read something. She's also asked her dear friends Al and Bonnie Paugh, but they couldn't make it.

When everyone had gotten there we all walked to the spot where Martha Jane had found Woody's body and formed a semi-circle looking out toward the water. It was cooler on the beach and Martha Jane had a very large bright red, pink and orange scarf type thing draped over her. It looked like something from India. She had asked us to dress up for the service which meant our clean jeans, and I put on the western shirt I'd gotten at Granny's which had belonged to Lottie's husband. Maggie wore a long, flowered skirt and she had a necklace made by Israel Shotridge, a famous Tlingit carver who lived on the island, and the other guys had on dress shirts with their jeans. Howie even had on a gray herringbone sports coat he'd gotten at Granny's.

Martha Jane started the service by reading, "I would like to begin by acknowledging that we gather today on the ancestral homelands of the Coast Salish and Suquamish Peoples. We acknowledge this with our deepest respect, honor, and gratitude to the Indigenous communities who have held relationship to this land and to the Salish Sea for generations."

A statement like this was often read at the beginning of a lot of events on the island. In fact, throughout our state, and some other states, too. Sometimes they say things about the shameful legacy of colonialism and their commitment to dismantle colonial practices. But I think Martha Jane didn't want to get off on too political a note. Not that she wasn't in agreement, but remembering the appalling details of what happened when the land was stolen would be a detour from the spirit she was hoping for in the memorial service.

Then she continued, "We are gathered here to recognize a man we will call Woody, a man not known to us, but a man brought by the tides which made Baker's Beach his resting place."

Then one by one, we followed her lead and each picked up a small rock from the beach and walked to the edge of the water and we said, "To Woody" and threw the rock in the water. After we each had done that, Walter picked up his ukulele from where he'd put it on a driftwood log and began to sing "Somewhere Over the Rainbow." It seems like you hear that at a lot of funerals these days, and I like it better than *Amazing Grace* with that line, "... and saved a poor wretch like me." I wouldn't like people to sing I was a poor wretch, even though I can relate to feeling like that sometimes. Walter sang,

> *"Somewhere over the rainbow*
> *Way up high ...*
> *And the dreams that you dream of*
> *Once in a lullaby ..."*

When he was done with the last verse about the lemon drops and the clouds, Martha Jane said, "Thank you Walter. That was beautiful, and I hope he will wake up where the clouds are far behind and the troubles melt like lemon drops." Then she turned to Howie, "We'll now have a reading. "No Man Is an Island," by John Donne. He lived in the late 1500's but I think we can all relate to it today." Then she nodded to Howie.

"No man is an island," he began, "every man is a piece of the continent ..."

While he read the poem, a gull hovered near the beach and let out several cries, sounds so mournful it was if the gull had come to grieve. "... Any man's death diminishes me, because I am involved in mankind.

And therefore never send to know for whom the bell tolls; it tolls for thee."

We were quiet for a minute; the only sounds were the gull and far across the water, the low motor of a tug pushing a barge.

"Thank you, Howie." Martha Jane reached under her big scarf and pulled a piece of paper from her pants pocket. "I've written a little something that I thought we can end on." She unfolded the paper and looked down at it, scowling. "Oh dear, I forgot my glasses."

"I'll read it, if you like." Howie held his hand out for the paper.

"Thank you. Your voice is better anyway." She smiled and handed it to him.

Martha Jane stood between me and Maggie and reached for our hands, and Maggie held Walter's hand and Walter held Mark's hand.

"Never will we know the life you led
Or those who may have hurt you,
Or those you may have hurt.
But this we know.
When you came into this world you were innocent.
A baby boy with his history not yet written.
You had a spirit, and a soul unmarked by life.
Today we honor that spirit.
And witness that you were here."

Howie put the paper down and held Mark's other hand. We all bowed our heads, and said "Amen." Then Walter played one last chorus of "Somewhere Over the Rainbow" and after that we left the beach and all headed back to Martha Jane's for cake and coffee.

I didn't stay long at Martha Jane's. I like everyone who was there, so that wasn't the problem. The people on Baker's Beach are pretty close, they do a lot of things together. And even though Bess and I lived up the road on the hill behind the beach, they often included us. And the cake was very good. Maggie made it; it was a triple chocolate cake, a round thing with a hole in the middle and just one layer with chocolate syrupy goo dripped over it. And there was coffee ice cream which was very good with the cake. Howie had brought some wine, too. It was a Merlot from Palouse Winery and although Martha Jane had made a pot of coffee, everyone except Walter went for the wine. Mark asked me how the Airbnb was doing and I was embarrassed to tell them the truth. It's humiliating to have to admit that this was the second time we had to pay a guest not to write a bad review. I knew I'd probably tell Martha Jane about the disaster with Carolyn Stein the next time we were alone, but with the group, I didn't want to get into it. I made some vague answer that there was a lot of competition on the island and we were just getting established. (Ha! Like getting established going down the toilet.) It's not that if I told the truth, they wouldn't be understanding. They were very kind; but it wouldn't be right to tell them I was going to quit, before I'd told Eddie. And also, the conversation had taken a serious turn—I suppose it was the wine and just coming from our service for Woody.

Death isn't exactly a light subject, even though sometimes at memorial services people who loved the dead person tell funny and charming stories about the person. But we didn't know Woody, and Walter wondered if he had taken his own life. And that led to a conversation about suicide. Mark said he had been depressed at various times in his life. He was very open about it and he talked about a therapist he saw during the height of the AIDS epidemic when he was losing so many friends. The therapist told him that in medicine there's an acceptance that some illnesses, like late stage cancer, can be terminal. But we never think that depression can be a terminal illness, when people kill themselves. Then Walter, who is a recovering alcoholic, talked about times in his life when he didn't want to go on. I left right after that because the conversation was getting me depressed. Not wanting to go on. I knew about that. I know about that.

It was really warm walking home away from the beach where it had been cooler. It felt more like midsummer. Although it never gets all that hot here. The average temperature in the spring is just in the high sixties. And in summer it's in the seventies. In fact, when it gets to eighty and above, which it does once in a while, everyone starts complaining. But not Bess. When it was hot she would sing—she had a beautiful voice. It never got weak and raspy as she aged, it was clear and true. Always.

I walked up the road from Baker's Beach and the sun warmed my face. Sunshine streamed through the deep green branches and warmth radiated from the gravel under my feet. It was so beautiful, it should have made me happy. I kept going—one foot in front of the other, trudging up the hill and I started to sweat. I squinted in the bright sunlight, squeezing my eyes together and I wished I had my sunglasses and then I thought about that sunshine song, the one about "sunshine on my shoulders makes me happy...sunshine in my eyes can make me cry." And I could hear her beautiful voice.

I didn't sing that one, George.

Really? Are you sure?

Of course.

So where did I get that?

John Denver sang it.

Oh, right. The guy that died in the plane crash. That was probably a quick way to go. Guns are messy.

Oh, George. You've got to keep going.

Nothing is really working out, Bess.

It's going to get better, believe me.

I wish I could. Bess, who sang the one you sang?

Lots of people. It's from Porgy and Bess.

Is that why you always sang it?

Not really.

Her voice faded. I couldn't find it and the road up the hill got steeper and as I was about ten yards from the house I heard an eagle. Eagles have an unmistakable sound, a high trilling like a flute that got stuck on a couple of notes. I looked way up in the trees on either side of the road, trying to locate it, but the sunshine hurt my eyes. And then, so clear and true ...

> *Summertime ... and the livin' is easy*
> *Fish are jumpin' and the cotton is high*
> *Oh, your daddy's rich and your ma is good-lookin'*
> *So hush, little baby, don't you cry*

I tried to talk, but there was no sound.

> *George, slow down a minute. Get your breath.*

I leaned against a fir tree on the side of the road. My breath kept catching, my voice wouldn't come. I wiped the sleeve of my cowboy shirt across my eyes.

> *It's going to get better, George.*

Hush little baby ... I hope you know how sorry I am we waited too long, Bess. We should have adopted. I know you wanted to.

> *We had a good life, George. And my cousin's kids were like ours—even better. We didn't have the baggage.*

I'm still so sorry that I dragged my feet. Sometimes I think all I wanted was you.

> *You play the hand you're dealt. Like Vinnie Barbarino the Seahawks coach used to say.*

Vinnie Barbarino was from "Welcome Back Kotter." The coach was Chuck Knox.

Oh, Chuck Knox, that's right. Now you listen to me, honey. It really is going to get better.

I didn't believe her. I wanted to tell her that, but she was gone.

BACK FROM MARTHA JANE'S

I KNEW THAT AS SOON AS I GOT HOME I WOULD HAVE TO face Eddie and tell him I was quitting the business, and it wasn't a happy thought. But the day was still beautiful and I tried very hard to do what Bess would want me to do: focus on the day's beauty and let go of the sadness that had rolled over me like a cold, salty wave when people talked about suicide at Martha Jane's. I stared at the forest and closed my eyes for a minute trying to get all the colors to fill my mind with something fresh and green and alive. The forest on either side of Baker's Beach Road was bright and sun drenched; it seemed like a warm, safe space as if at any minute the Seven Dwarfs would be marching through the trees singing, "Hi-ho, Hi-ho." They were good guys those dwarfs. They had a good attitude, singing the way they did as they went off to work. My mother took me to that movie not long after my Dad left. (I didn't tell my friends because I was afraid they would think it was babyish. I was ten and going to a movie, especially one based on a fairy tale—just you and your Mom— was *not* cool.) But I really liked those dwarfs. I could relate to all of them, except maybe Doc. But I knew what it was like being sleepy, grumpy, bashful and happy and although I didn't sneeze a lot, I could relate to Sneezy, too. They seemed decent and I would have liked to have guys like that on my side. I appreciated the way they had Snow White's back. Mom was trying so hard to be there for me, so when she suggested we see the movie, I couldn't say no. She tried to just let me be a kid. At least until she got sick.

I don't have many memories about when my Dad left; all I knew was that he'd been fired for being drunk, and I think my Mom said he went to a place to quit drinking. It must have been a rehab place, although you didn't hear that much about those programs back then. Years later, on a TV channel that ran old movies, I saw the *Days of Wine and Roses* and there was a frightening scene with Jack Lemmon going through delirium tremors, DT's. He was hallucinating, just shaking and screaming with pure terror. It made me wonder if that's what happened to my dad. If quitting was so horrible that he couldn't take it and just went back to drinking (which is what Lee Remick did in the movie). And then because he couldn't quit, he never came back to us.

I can't say I really missed him; it was better without him. My mother was less anxious, not that she was happy—but not sad and tense all the time. I suppose what I did miss was the idea of a father. There weren't many divorced people back then—at least not in our neighborhood, and there was a shame and stigma that I know she felt. We both did. I was the only kid in my class without a father and it made me feel different— because I was. Not that people went out of their way to make me feel bad about it, but it was there. I carried it around. I'm sure it was worse for my mother; she was a woman whose husband had walked out on her and no matter what a loser he was, that made people wonder about her. What was wrong with her? Why couldn't she hold on to her man? Blaming her. Or if not that, at best she was an object of pity.

I felt terrible for her when the cancer became terminal, when she was dying—but I was a coward. I did everything to avoid her, something I'm still ashamed of—even though I've tried to tell myself I was just a kid and Bess said I should forgive myself— but I haven't been able to.

I was on the cross country team and I remember running for miles, just running and running. I'd run through the arboretum, and all along Lake Washington Boulevard next to the lake as far as you could go. I told her I had to practice, even when I didn't. I lied about it and left for hours. The only thing I looked forward to was seeing Bess at school and there have been times I've wondered if I ever really grieved for Mom—I was so wrapped up in Bess.

After Mom died and I was living at the Braxton's, I went to church with them. Mrs. Braxton would sit between me and Bess and that's when I first heard Bess sing. What a beautiful voice. I think the people who were in hospice were really lucky to have had Bess in that group that sang for them. One of the women in the group, Mrs. Wainwright had a harp (I forgot her first name) but it was an actual big harp that she'd roll in on a narrow platform. The people who were dying loved the harp, except for one man who Bess said sat up and yelled, "Get that fucking harp out of here!" But he was the exception.

I'm not sure what music I'd want if I was on the

way out. Maybe Marvin Gaye singing "What's Going On." I have to say dying is something I think about. But not the way most people my age think about their mortality. For me, it's the feeling sometimes of just not wanting to go on. Bess would never forgive me if I did end my own life. But I have to say I can imagine how people could do it. How they could be in so much pain that they'd lose sight of hurting loved ones. I'm not there. Not even close. But that doesn't mean I can't imagine it. Maybe get in a kayak and just keep paddling, and you'd get numb from the cold and just fade away and you'd slip into a watery grave like Puff the Magic Dragon, and then Puff came no more. Mom used to sing that, she had a beautiful voice like Bess.

As I walked up the hill, I got closer to the house, which meant I was closer to telling Eddie I was done. I went over it in my mind repeating, "I quit, Eddie." Repeating it like a mantra, over and over again so I wouldn't get hooked and drawn into any protests he'd make. It's strange how what's on your mind changes how you see things. Practicing what I'd say to Eddie was unpleasant and it was like a switch had flipped. Now the sky, although still blue, looked distant and cold and the lush green forest seemed vulnerable, as if at any minute it could be ravaged by fire and turned into a desolate wasteland where nothing grew. It makes me wonder about what reality is, when emotions can change the way things appear.

When I got home, Eddie wasn't there. It was actually a relief—but not a reprieve. I'd still have to tell him. I didn't know when he'd be back and I didn't want to call him to find out, so I got a beer and plopped down in the plaid chair. I don't know how long I sat there drinking beer and poking the hole where the stuffing came out. What made my gloom so difficult was that I thought I had been making progress. I had been able glimpse a future where there might be breaks from the loneliness. A flicker of possibility that I could carve out some kind of life that would feel like it was better than just existing. But now I was starting to feel like I was back to square one, stuck again in a revolving door of grief.

The Airbnb was hopeless. I knew what Eddie would say—that he was sure we'd get more guests. But if we ever did get any new guests, it would most likely lead to another fiasco. I could just see it. I pictured an old, retired couple, probably my age, a trial lawyer who had been with one of the fancy law firms where they made you pay $5000 up front and then $400 or $500 an hour, and his wife was also a retired lawyer who had made a ton of money. And the only reason they ended up at Bluebell Nook was because they'd come to the island on a whim and all the other Airbnb's were full. And after arriving, on their way to the basement room, the wife tripped and broke her ankle and they sued us for negligence because the night before a branch had broken and some twigs had littered the path. And then because Eddie and I could only afford a crappy lawyer, the people naturally won the lawsuit. Then I had to sell the house to pay them and now I was living under an I-5 bridge in Seattle.

As I thought about it, I decided it would be better to do more than just telling him "I quit" over and over. I should make sure Eddie got the message about why I was quitting the business, and after I gave him the facts, then I could repeat "I quit" to anything he said to try to talk me out of it. I went to the desk and got out all the receipts for what we'd bought to show him how much money we were losing.

> Business license Application fee – $19
> Business License – $90
> Two sets of Queen size sheets – $72.39
> Two sets of towels – $40.99
> Box of fancy soap – $17.99
> Velveeta cheese –$4.98
> Fig Newtons – $3.99
> Cabernet – $12
> Chardonnay –$15
> Small refrigerator – $94.80
> Tillamook Cheddar Cheese – $9.95
> Scottie's singing – $25
> Smart Mouse Trap – $10.99
> Misc. Expense – $160 ($75 to O'Grady's and $85 to C.
> Stein not to write bad review)
> Service fee to Airbnb 3% for 3 guests – $6.30

I totaled it up (I decided not to add the cost of the Triscuits because I ate most of them or the Cheez Whiz because we only used it the one time and it made a mess) and it all came to $583.38. And our income was $0.00 from the first two guests because we had to refund their money, and Molly paid us $70 for the one night she was here. So we were in the hole $513.38. And actually it was even more because he bought grapes and more wine and I don't know what that cost.

While I was at the desk I realized I'd lost track of

how long it had been since I'd checked for emails and I decided I'd better look—all the while hoping there wouldn't be any. I was relieved when I saw we only had one. But then my heart did something weird. When you're young and your heart flutters, you think it's because you're afraid or excited, but when you're old, you think you have atrial fibrillation and you might need a pace maker—or some meds that you have to stay on for the rest of your life—that is, if you don't have a stroke that totally zaps your brain. But since I'd never had weird heart flutters before, I was pretty sure it was the same as a young person: fear or excitement. And as I looked at the email, it wasn't either/or. Fear or excitement—it was both. The email was from Molly. And I didn't know what to think—I remembered again how she said that stuff about being on a plane with a stranger you'd never see again, and how she'd left in a rush without saying a thing about wanting to come back. How hard would it have been to just say a few words? "I'd like to come back, I'll email you." But that didn't happen and it didn't take me long to realize I'd been a fool to imagine that our time together meant anything to her. And why would it? I'm an old geezer and I can't think of what I have to offer a woman, in spite of what I know Bess would say. So I'd quit hoping. It wasn't hard.

Hi George and Eddie,

I wanted to see if I could book with you for next weekend for the night of the 5th. It'll just be me, and I'd aim for the 6:30 ferry from Pt. Defiance and get there early evening. If you're booked for that

weekend, if you could let me know another weekend
this month that could work, that would be great.

Thanks,

Molly Gorman

I guess the island made a pretty big hit. I read her
email again. At least three times. It was straightforward,
very clear: she wanted to come back. I don't know why
it confused me. Many people find the island remarkable. They're surprised that 20 minutes by ferry from
two very urban cities there's this beautiful, peaceful
place without a single traffic light or a Starbucks or
McDonald's. A place with farms and sheep, horses,
goats, and also other creatures like eagles, ospreys,
deer and occasionally, where even orca whales can
be seen swimming by. And then the views—views of
two mountain ranges, the Olympics and the Cascades,
to say nothing of the magnificent Mt. Rainer—why
wouldn't she want to come back for that?

I read it again. It was addressed to both me and
Eddie. Nothing confusing about that: she'd met us
both. We were interchangeable. I wasn't any different
from Eddie—we were the proprietors of Bluebell Nook.
Although it was my house. But she knew that, and she
didn't want to leave Eddie out, or she wanted to make
a point that I was just the innkeeper guy. Just an innkeeper guy, like Eddie was an innkeeper guy. Nothing
special. Nothing more than that. My mind went round
and round. It was pathetic.

I couldn't tell her that Bluebell Nook was closing

before I'd even told Eddie. I'd have to put off my conversation with him, but I'd still have to have it because
one guest, no matter how often she came, wasn't enough
to keep the business going. We were the only Airbnb on
the island without a single review. And although we'd
escaped the O'Grady's and Carolyn Stein writing bad
ones, having zero reviews still sent the message that no
one came here. It's like an empty restaurant makes you
think there's something wrong with the food. I'd reply
and confirm her reservation this time, but the day after
she left, I'd tell Eddie it was over.

> Hi Molly,
> You're all set for the night of the 5th—see you then.
> George and Eddie

Signing it from both of us would let her know that
I understood that to her I was just an innkeeper guy.
But then I thought I should sign something besides just
our names. So I changed it and typed:

> Best,
> George and Eddie

Then I thought that wasn't friendly enough, so I
deleted it and instead signed it:

> Cheers,
> George and Eddie

We'd have to get the basement room ready. It hadn't
been touched since the disaster with Carolyn Stein, but
I didn't feel like dealing with it. Not at all. Everything

that had been happening had set me back: Molly leaving without a word; Carolyn Stein screaming about wild animals and wanting her money back; Eddie getting a gun; and the memorial on the beach for Woody (when everyone talked about death and suicide). It was all too much. But it had to be done, so I called Eddie— no way I was getting that room ready myself.

"We've got another guest, Eddie. Don't get excited, I think it's our swan song."

"I told you we'd recover. You always think the glass is half empty."

"Half empty? There's NO glass!"

"You're so negative."

"Well, you have to get over here and help me get the room ready."

"I've been very focused on tracking the killer of the chicken, George."

"Big friggin' deal. I don't even like the chickens. Don't weasel out of this, Eddie. I've seen this movie before."

"Look, how 'bout this—you get the room ready, and after the guest leaves, I'll do all the clean up and get the room ready for the next one."

"There's probably not going to be a next one. And I don't get why you can't come now."

"Lottie just got a cord of wood delivered and I promised I'd stack it for her."

"Oh, all right. The hell with it."

"Who's the guest?"

"Molly. The woman from Portland."

"The one you think is gay?"

"She's not. I got it wrong."

"Well, it's repeat business! That's the best. You develop

a clientele and they come back year after year—repeat business is a goldmine!"

I wanted to say, "And how'd that work out for those gold miners who went to Alaska and froze to death." But I stuffed it—maybe I had been too negative.And Eddie said again that he'd do the cleaning after Molly left so I hung up. He sure was spending quite a bit of time at Lottie's. He was hardly around and that would be another thing I could point out about why I was quitting this partnership.

I really didn't want to face the guest room, it was probably littered with mice turds and if the towels had been left wet, they could be getting moldy, making the whole room smell like mildew. I'm usually primed to expect the worst, but I was surprised when I took the vacuum, mop, the bucket of cleaning supplies, and the fresh sheets and towels to the basement. The Smart Mouse Trap was empty and there weren't any turds. Maybe the word had gotten out in the mouse community that Bluebell Nook was a place to avoid. Even the used towels weren't in a wet heap on the bathroom floor. The room really wasn't bad.

I started in the bathroom and gathered up the towels and piled them by the door. I always did the bathroom first to get it over with. After I cleaned the toilet, shower and sink and mopped the bathroom floor, I dusted everything in the bedroom and vacuumed. Then I stripped the sheets and dumped them by the door with the towels. I hadn't wanted to spend that much money on sheets and towels, but Eddie had

insisted and I could see his point. We had several sets,
both were a buttery yellow color that was very cheerful.
The color was a lot like Martha Jane's kitchen. And the
sheets were silky soft. I took them over to the bed.

I didn't want to think about who would be sleeping
in this room. But thoughts kept popping into my head
like crazy and persistent robocalls.

(She liked this room or she wouldn't have wanted
to come back.)

(Forget her. Just make the damn bed.)

(Pretend this room is for a stranger.)

(Not like someone I'd met before.)

(Someone easy to talk to—about mice and movies.)

(And about losing a spouse and getting old.)

(Who laughed at my dumb jokes.)

(And had a nightgown like Bess's from LL Bean.)

(Would that be too warm?)

(Maybe a Ducks tee shirt.)

(Or the Portland Thorns. A blue one. Like her eyes.)

(How would it come off? Would she?)

(Or … Is it like riding a bike?)

(Of course if your legs are too wobbly you can't pedal ...)

WHAT THE HELL WAS I DOING? Here I was going from assuming that Molly had no interest in me, to imagining what kind of nightgown she wore! And how it would come off! Get a grip! Quit thinking about her. Quit hoping.

> *Everyone needs hope, George.*

But if you hope and it goes south, it's better that you never hoped.

> *You just need confidence.*

That you can make things happen?

> *Not that. Not thinking you can control things, but that that you can handle whatever happens.*

If it turns out she doesn't want anything to do with me. Could I handle that?

> *Of course you could, George.*

I feel weak and silly.

> *You're not. Not at all.*

You always say nice things, Bess.

> *Because it's true. You've handled a lot of tough things.*

I don't know about that.

Of course you have. Your father's drinking, walking out when you were ten.

That wasn't a day in the park.

Right. And you were only sixteen when your Mom died.

But you were there then, Bess.

But you got through it.

I don't know if I could have without you and your family.

Look, George—you've kept going these past two years, and it hasn't been easy.

You got that right.

You can handle whatever happens. I know this about you.

I started to tell her that I didn't know that. I didn't have confidence that I could handle whatever happens. I wanted to hear her say it again. Maybe it could sink in, even a little. But I couldn't get her voice and hear her anymore. She wasn't there.

I put the throw pillows on the bed, picked up the pile of sheets and towels and left.

THE GUN

MOLLY WAS SUPPOSED TO GET THE 6:30 BOAT FROM PT. Defiance. If the boat was on time, she would arrive at the latest by 7:15. I sat in the plaid chair looking out the window. I was not relaxed. It was like the waiting room at the clinic, when you sit there thinking about all the things that might be wrong with you. And you can't concentrate on the old magazines they have. Like *People*, where even if you could concentrate it wouldn't help because you don't know who any of the people are in *People*. Or if you look at your phone to read the news, you can't concentrate on that either. I even wished Eddie was here to talk to, which might have taken my mind off how stupid I felt to imagine that someone as cool as Molly would like me. It was like high school. That's exactly how it felt. Where there were all these cute girls—the pretty, peppy ones that just sparkled as they waltzed down the halls—and you were a nobody to them. Like you might as well have been one of the dull gray lockers, flat against the walls that everyone just passed by.

And talk about high school, Eddie was still spending a lot of time helping Lottie at her place and he seemed kind of teenage-y to me, the way he wasn't around all that much and just came home at night to sleep.

Every few minutes I looked at my watch, which certainly didn't help the time go any faster. It was ridiculous. Then I remembered how we'd sat in the living room and had beer and Fig Newtons and Velveeta. Maybe this time, if she still wanted to have a drink— she might want wine. I went in the kitchen to check. We had both red and white: a bottle of Merlot and a bottle of Chardonnay. I didn't know which she'd prefer, and I put the Chardonnay in the refrigerator. But if she wanted that, it might take a while to get cold. So I put in the freezer. The wine glasses looked kind of dusty, so I decided to wash them. And I noticed the kitchen looked pretty grubby; the sink was gucky and the counters were kind of sticky so I got some Krud Kutter and started frantically squirting it all over everything and scrubbing away. By now it was 7:35 and I was sure she wasn't coming. I threw the Krud Kutter under the sink and went back to the plaid chair.

The boat at Pt. Defiance had probably been really late and she went over to Anthony's restaurant near the ferry dock to get a drink while she waited. And a guy in his seventies who worked out all the time and was thin, but muscular, and who had a lot of hair, sat next to her. They struck up a conversation and hit it off. Big time. Like the sky lit up with fireworks and bells rang. It was love at first sight and he convinced her to leave the ferry line and follow him in his classic, forest green Porche to his penthouse condo at Ruston overlooking Commencement Bay.

But would Molly do that without cancelling her reservation? She might forget to cancel if she was swept off her feet. But I thought I should check the computer, just in case even though it felt futile. Everything felt dark and heavy. Even if there wasn't the buff guy with the full head of hair at Anthony's, she probably had something come up a lot more interesting than Bluebell Nook. The gloom that saturated me was different than right after Bess died; it wasn't the intense pain like you'd just had your leg cut off. This was a dead numbness. Just empty. They say that when a person has a leg amputated, they feel like it's still there. I think it's like that for me with Bess.

Like a robot, I scrolled through the email. There were ads for all kinds of things: Freedom Mortgage, 5G Male Sex Help, Silver Singles, Technik Smartwatch, Citizens Gold Trust, Budget Blinds, Motion Glo LED Light Bar, eharmony, Full Auto Coverage, Keranique for Hair Loss, Liberty Mutual Pet Insurance, 123inkjets, Bath&Shower Pros—to name just a few. I wondered how some of these places got our email. Especially the Male Sex Help, Silver Singles, eharmony and the one for hair loss. Must have been Eddie's doing. All those companies trying to get our money was annoying, and I didn't see anything from Molly.

I was shutting off the computer when I heard a knock on the door. I ran to the window. The blue Prius!

A switch flipped. Like night and day. A different planet. Everything was bright and light. "This little light of mine / let it shine / let it shine / let it shine" … "Jesus wants me for a sunbeam" … I flung open the door.

"Hi, George." Molly grinned. She put down her bag and gave me a quick, friendly hug. The top of her head was right under my chin and even though the hug was quick, I could feel her warmth against me. She drew back and we let go (I didn't want to) and she smiled. "The ferry was late, hope that wasn't a problem."

"Oh no. It happens a lot." It's weird when the words that come out of your mouth are no match for what's been in your head. How I'd been convinced she wasn't coming and that everything was no good—and then she shows up and BAM! Boo ... *YAY!* Dark ... *LIGHT!*

What am I? A hollow table lamp that other people switch on and off?

("This little light of mine" ... "Jesus wants me for a sunbeam?" Where had that come from? Sunday school? "Dropkick me Jesus Through the Goalposts of Life." That was actually a real song. Although not sung in Sunday school.)

My mind raced with stupid stuff. I just bounced around. And what was the hug about? She probably would have hugged Eddie the same way. She was a friendly person, and hugs can be like handshakes. No big deal.

Get a grip, George.

I'm a mess, Bess.

That sounds like a country song. Just offer her a drink.

Then what?

Whatever.

Okay. I took a deep breath. Whatever.

"Would you like a drink? We have some wine now."
"That'd be great. Thanks." Molly took off her parka and lay it over her bag.

"Here, I'll take that." I grabbed her parka and scurried to hang it on one of the hooks by the door. "Just have a seat, I'll be right there."

She smiled and went to the couch in front of the fireplace where she'd sat the last time. People usually do that. They go to the same seat they had before. I wonder why that is? Creatures of habit, or is it something like claiming territory? Do men do that more than women? Dogs pee on territory. But not female dogs, I don't think. At least not so much. Or do they?

Get the wine, George.

Oh, right.

Look, you're just nervous.

You were always perceptive, Bess.

Ask her if she wants red or white.

Oh, right. I forgot that.

I tried to do my imitation of a good host. "So, Molly— would you like red or white? We have Merlot and Chardonnay."

"Chardonnay, thanks." Her smile knocked me out. Her blue eyes crinkled and there was something pixie-like about her face with her short, silky looking white hair. And I noticed that Molly was *very* pretty. I had known she was attractive in this sturdy, outdoor, athletic way. I had noticed that before—but now? She looked so pretty—why now? I didn't think she'd had a facelift. She wasn't the type, not being one to wear make-up—at least it didn't look like it when I saw her before. Those things didn't seem to go together: not wearing make-up and getting a facelift. But what did I know? I shook my head and opened the freezer to get the Chardonnay. Damn. It had started to freeze.

I took it to the sink and quickly ran it under the water—and then the bottle cracked and it slipped out of my hand. "Shit!" When I went to pick up a chunk of the glass, I was in such a rush, it sliced my palm. I stared at the blood dripping in the sink on top of the broken bottle. I must have yelled again because Molly rushed in the kitchen.

"You've got a nasty cut there." She took my hand and then grabbed a paper towel and held it to the cut.

"Would you like Merlot? The blood's same color."

She laughed. "Where do you keep your first-aid stuff? Let me take care of this."

"It's not a big deal. It's in the bathroom—I can get it." But I didn't move. She was standing close to me and holding my hand, while she pressed the paper towel over the cut. It was another thing that didn't match: words and action. The words said that I could get the first-aid stuff, but I didn't move. I couldn't get in gear. I didn't want to leave her. I looked down at her and shook my head, like someone trying to focus and come back to earth. "The bathroom is a mess. It's embarrassing and I don't want you to see it."

"I'm not a stranger to messy bathrooms, or messy anything." She smiled, looking up at me. I wanted to kiss her.

"It's okay. I'll be right back." I trotted off to the

bathroom, pulling myself together. There wasn't a Band-Aid long enough for the cut, so I got a piece of gauze, wrapped it around my palm and taped it. I looked in the bathroom mirror. Thinning gray hair, Shnauzery eyebrows, faded brown-eyes, a lined, craggy face with sagging jowls and a double-chin. What was I thinking? Imagining kissing that pretty woman. "Pretty woman don't walk on by / Pretty woman don't make me cry."

I looked down at the sink. I'm losing it. I'm really losing it.

No you're not.

What was I thinking, Bess?

You're just nervous.

It was dumb to put the wine in the freezer.

Yes, it was.

I saw myself in the mirror. What a joke.

You're still handsome.

Only you would say that.

Not true. I know about this. Go back to her.

I feel ridiculous.

Just get her a glass of the other wine.

What if she doesn't want it?

Offer her a beer.

A beer. Oh, right. Like the last time.

Right. You can do this, George.

When I got to the kitchen, Molly had cleaned up all the glass. "Oh, you didn't need to do that."

"Not a problem."

"Well, thanks. Another Bluebell Nook fiasco, I'm afraid."

She laughed. "Shall we try again?"

She had a great laugh, and that made me smile. "Absolutely. Would you like Merlot? Or we have beer, too."

"I'll have the Merlot. Might as well."

"I'll bring it to you. You're supposed to be the guest."

She touched my arm and smiled up at me and then went back to the living room. I uncorked the wine and poured us each a glass, reminding myself that she was a warm, friendly person and that I shouldn't read any more into it.

In the living room I handed her the wine and started to sit across from her, but I realized I hadn't brought any food. "Can I get you something to eat? I'm not sure what we have but—"

"The wine is great. I stopped in Olympia on the way up and got a bite."

"You're sure—I could see if we have—"

"Really this is fine, thanks."

I sat across from her and I couldn't think of anything to say, so I asked about the weather. "How's it been in Portland? ... The weather—how's it been?"

"Oh. The weather. Well, it's been nice. Usually it's a little warmer than up here. My neighbors have all been out working in their gardens."

I sipped my wine, "Do you like that?"

"The wine's lovely."

"I mean gardening. Do you like to garden?"

She laughed. "I love being outside, but not to do work. I know the people who love gardening don't really consider it work, at least not in a bad way. Work can be great if you love what you're doing. But growing up on a farm, there was so much I had to do. Both my sister and I didn't have much free time, we were always working with our parents." She took a sip of her wine. "What about you?"

"I did the usual. You know—mowed the lawn, took out the garbage, helped with the dishes. That kind of thing. But I took on more after my dad left—when my parents split up."

I never talk about my Dad. It bothered me the way it just popped out. I poked at the stuffing in the chair and quickly asked, "What did you grow on your farm?"

"Blueberries, but also vegetables—tomatoes, peppers, eggplant, pole and bush green beans, onions, cucumbers, summer squash and beets. And we raised chickens. It was a ton of work and almost every minute we weren't in school we were working. But it got too much for my folks after my sister and I went to college, so they sold it." She sipped her wine. "Do you have any brothers or sisters?"

"No, just me. Same with Bess. We're both 'onlys.' I don't think it was as common then. Nowadays there seem to be more people who just have one kid. Is your sister in Portland?"

"San Francisco. We see each other about once a year and talk on the phone every few weeks. I suppose we're close in our way. I mean we'd always help each other, and after our father died, our mother needed a lot of support so we'd spell each other. And we were both with her when she died." Molly was quiet for a minute, then she asked, "You said your dad left? Were your parents divorced?"

We'd been talking quietly and it was comfortable, like eating macaroni and cheese while wearing an old pair of sweats, or a chocolate-chip cookie straight from the oven. She was making me think of food. I could jump up and see if we had any Triscuits. Or ask her again about her farm. All those berries and vegetables. Just change the subject. I was good at that. But I didn't.

"He was an alcoholic and he left after he got fired."

"Just up and left?"

"Yep. What a guy."

"That must have been rough, how old were you?"

"Ten. But honestly, he left a lot to be desired in the father department. So I don't think I was scarred for life."

She smiled. "No, I don't think so."

"You don't?" I tried to keep it casual, but I had this little tingly thing going in my chest.

"Not that I've noticed."

"Well, you don't really know me."

"But I'd like to get to know you better." She laughed. Light and easy and I think she may have even winked, but I'm not sure. "I had a wonderful time when I was here before. I wanted to bring Aggie, but when I told my stepson I'd be gone this weekend, my granddaughter Shannon begged to have her stay with them. Would you like to see their picture?"

"I would. And I'll get more wine." I came back from the kitchen with the bottle of Merlot, and put it on the coffee table and sat next to her.

Molly got her phone from her purse, scrolled through the photos and then handed it to me. My face was close to hers as we looked at the photo of a smiling young girl, sitting on a step next to a big fluffy dog. She had one arm around the dog and rested her cheek against the top of its head.

"The dog is beautiful, and your granddaughter, too. How old she?"

"Shannon is twelve, and I'm not sure about Aggie since she's a rescue. But I think she might be around four."

I didn't want to move away from her. "Do you have more photos of them?"

"Tons." She started scrolling though the photos, but looked up because just then Eddie burst in the room. Not only did he spoil the mood, but he looked ridiculous—he was waving his gun.

"I think I *got* it!" he shouted. Then he noticed Molly. "Oh, hello, um … "

"Molly," she reminded him of her name as she looked at the gun. "Been hunting?"

"I guess George didn't tell you."

"I wasn't hiding it, Eddie." He sounded like I was trying to pull something over on her and I found that very annoying. "It just didn't come up."

"Didn't tell me what?" Molly said, smiling. "Now I'm curious."

Eddie put the gun down. "Our last guest, really

thought it was great here. She'd spent time in Scotland, and she had some family who lived there and she often visited them, but then she had a hip replacement and you can get blood clots on long flights from that so her doctor didn't want her to travel so she came here to get a little taste of Scotland. She was crazy about our singer, Scottie. They really hit it off and sang together—"

"Get to the point, Eddie."

"Right. Okay. Well, everything was great but in the middle of the night she screamed her head off because something came and killed one of our chickens—"

"*My* chickens."

"Right. George's chickens and she went out to see what the commotion was and she saw whatever killed the chicken run off and it left the bloody thing right by her door."

"What did you think it was?" Molly asked. "A raccoon, or a coyote?"

"She said it was big, so it could have been either of those. But we've also had cougars on the island," Eddie said, solemnly. "So every night I've been out trying to track it and tonight about fifty yards from the back of the house, I saw something big moving and I took aim, shot, and it took off! I grazed it, but I sent a message all right."

"It was the second time a guest wanted their money back," I added. "So of course, we gave her a full refund. And a little something not to write a bad review."

Eddie nodded. "Having a dead chicken by the guest room door, all bloody and everything isn't good for business."

Just then the front door flew open and Lottie charged

in, pointing her finger at Eddie and yelling, "WHAT HAVE YOU DONE! *Just look at this!*"

Eddie froze. Molly and I stood up and stared. Behind Lottie was her dog Max who was covered in bright blue splotches.

"Oh my God," Eddie hit himself in the forehead. "I shot *Max*!"

"What's that all over him?" I stared at the dog.

"It's from my gun. Oh my God, I'm so sorry Lottie!"

"What are you talking about?" I looked over at Eddie, who held his head in his hands.

"My gun. It's a paintball gun." Eddie shook his head. "I wanted to scare it—not kill it."

"I think that's very commendable," Molly sat back down on the couch.

Lottie spun around and glared at Molly. "Who are you?"

"Molly Gorman. I'm staying here at Bluebell Nook."

Eddie gestured toward Lottie. "This is my friend, Lottie." he said politely to Molly, trying to make a nice introduction.

Lottie glared at him. "*Friend?* You have lot of nerve Eddie—just look at what you've done to Max!" She got down on the floor and knelt next to the dog, stroking his head and making little baby cooing noises.

Eddie went to her and bent down, putting his hand on her shoulder. "Please let me make it up to you. I'll wash him and pay for any vet bills or grooming. Whatever he needs." He leaned closer to her. "I'm so sorry, Lottie."

"This paint better not hurt him!" she snarled. "Just look at this blue crap stuck all over his beautiful coat."

"It's non-toxic. It said so right on the label."

"Yeah, well it better be." She stroked Max's head, murmuring more little cooing noises. Then Eddie kneeled next to her and put his arm around her shoulder, and she let him hold her for a minute.

"Lottie, I was hunting the cougar, or coyote, or whatever it was. You said you keep Max in at night," he reminded her.

"He has to go out to pee!" she snapped.

"I'm so sorry," Eddie apologized again, and then patted Max. "I'm sorry, Max. I didn't mean to shoot you. Let me help you with him, Lottie."

She just glared at him. Then finally, still very irked, she said, "Oh, all right, if you insist."

"I insist."

She tried to stand up, but she scowled and seemed stuck so Eddie got up, offered his hand and helped Lottie to her feet. "I know you can't lift him into that big washtub. He's too heavy for you. I'll take care of it."

Lottie sighed. "Poor Max."

"He'll be clean and looking great," Eddie reassured her, "I promise, Lottie." And then, ignoring us, the three of them went to the door and left.

"Well, that was a little excitement," I said, as soon as they were gone.

"I'll say."

"I'm really sorry about all that, Molly. More wine?"

"Sure. Just a tad, thanks." She held out her glass. "I'm glad it wasn't a real gun."

I filled her glass halfway. "I don't much care for them myself."

"Lottie's dog will be okay. Paint ball guns are popular with kids, teenagers mostly I think. And I'm sure the paint is harmless."

"I hope so. Max is everything to Lottie—he's her family. A while back he used to come around my place and harass the chickens. And right after Bess died I was really pissed off about it. I yelled at her, told her to keep her damn dog out of my yard. She did try to keep him in at night after that, but I'd upset her. My yelling at her like that."

"It's hard to imagine, you seem pretty calm to me."

"I suppose I am mostly. But after Bess died, it didn't take much. I was angry at everything." I didn't like remembering those days when I hated the world and everything in it. I looked at my drink, trying to think of something else to say but couldn't come up with anything.

Molly was quiet, too. But after a few minutes she said, "I can remember that kind of anger. When anything can set you off," she paused, then said, quietly. "It was like that when my mother died. She died of breast cancer and it came at a time when Dennis and I weren't doing that well. Tommy, my stepson was a teenager and he was a real handful. He and Dennis always went at it and the tension seemed to poison everything."

"I hate tension. Probably had too much of it before my dad left, so I think I let a lot of things go. For me—not that much is worth fighting about."

"Were you happy? You and Bess?"

"Yes, I'd say so, although I think there can be one person who loves more than the other, and that one would be me. And for men my age, we don't have the

really close friends like women do, so we're pretty depen-
dent on women. What about you? And your husband?"

"Time helped, so when Tommy was in college
things were better. But Dennis was in charge and there
wasn't a lot of give and take. I just adapted to it and it
probably took its toll. I had a suspicious mammogram
recently, something my doctor just wants to watch.
I'm supposed to go back for another one in a couple of
months. With my family history it's a worry—I guess
that's why I'm so determined to pay attention to what
I want. How *I* want to spend my time." She laughed,
"And I'm getting pretty good at it. This morning my
stepson asked me at the last minute if I'd come over
and stay with Shannon. His wife was going to a jewelry party, whatever that is, and he had some kind of
meeting about fantasy football. And I said, 'No.' It felt
wonderful and I'm getting better at it."

"Good for you, I don't think it's always that easy
to change."

"It isn't, but I think it starts with small things. Not
some huge change of direction, but focusing on something that is just a little different than what you might
usually do. In the past I would have changed my plans
to accommodate him. This time I didn't—of course
if it had been a real emergency I would have helped
out. But for jewelry shopping and fantasy football?"
She grinned. "I just wasn't going to give up my plans—
especially since he didn't give me any notice. I do have
to go back tomorrow afternoon, so it might seem silly
to come for just the one night, but I wanted to be here
again. This place seems to speak to me." Molly looked

at her watch. "Well, I guess I'd better turn in." She took her wine glass into the kitchen.

"You don't need to do that," I said, following her with my glass and the bottle. "You're supposed to be the guest."

She laughed again. "I actually feel like a friend, George."

"Me, too." Our eyes met so I asked, "How 'bout if I walk you down to your room?"

"Sure." She nodded and went to the door and I took her parka off the hook. I didn't know if I should help her on with it and take her bag. The other time when I'd offered, she said she didn't need any help. She saw me hesitate, so she took her parka from me and then I reached for her bag.

I walked behind her and the path itself was well lit from the outdoor light, but everything else on either side was dark. The night air was crisp and cool and there wasn't much wind. The moon was just a sliver, but the dark sky was studded with stars. Above us we heard the hoot of an owl.

"An owl." Molly whispered.

"We often hear them." I whispered, as I followed her down the path.

"Why are we whispering?"

"I dunno. You did, so I did."

She looked back at me and I could see her beautiful smile. "It's so incredibly quiet here. I guess I didn't want to disturb it."

At the door I handed her bag to her. She took it and instead of opening the door, she set it down.

Talk about high school! I froze. What exactly was I

supposed to do? What did it mean—her setting her bag down like that? Was this a signal and I was supposed to ask if I could come in the room? What if that was what she wanted, and then I fizzled and she mentioned Viagra with a laugh and I tried to laugh, too, but I couldn't laugh because I felt so ridiculous.

Molly looked up and sighed, "Oh, I think I just saw a shooting star."

I lifted my head and stared at the starlit sky. I wasn't quick enough to see the shooting star, but I kept looking up. I could see the Milky Way and the Big Dipper and I wondered what satellites might be spinning around up there. I found Polaris—the bright North Star, and then the Little Dipper. The vastness and beauty of the universe made me feel insignificant in a way that was mysteriously peaceful. I don't know if calm is anywhere near brave, but when my gaze left the night sky, my eyes looked into hers and held there. "Molly ... can I kiss you?"

She moved toward me and gently held my face with her soft hands. Her lips were warm and yielding and the tenderness and sweetness were almost more than I could bear. I put my arms around her and drew her to me and felt my eyes moist with tears. Then we just held each other. We stayed like that, standing at the foot of the path outside her door underneath the starry sky, holding each other for a long time before we said goodnight.

MOLLY'S LAST DAY

AFTER WE SAID GOODNIGHT, MOLLY DIDN'T ASK ME TO come in which was actually a relief since I'd had those embarrassing fears. Before I went to bed, I'd thought about having another glass of wine, but decided against it because sometimes it messes up my sleep. I turned out the lights in the kitchen and living room, got ready for bed and turned in. But I didn't sleep. I lay there jazzed, gazing at the ceiling. All I could think about was Molly in bed in the room beneath me. And I imagined being there with her and the whole idea of it made me feel alive, vigorous— young even—not the balding, paunchy old fart that I am. Wondering if she could really care for me kept my mind stuck in a flashing montage of conflicting thoughts: she likes me/the kiss meant nothing ... she likes me/the kiss meant nothing. And on and on until I gave up, flipped on the light and tried to read. It was a novel by an Alaska writer that I like a lot. But I kept reading the same paragraph over and over, so I put it down and tried again to sleep.

Finally, I did fall asleep, but Molly was firmly planted in my brain and I dreamed of her. I wonder if it's common for old people to have dreams about their youth. Their glory days. Not that I had any of those—no great moments on the football field, or being elected president of the class, or taking a gorgeous cheerleader to the prom. No sex, drugs and rock n' roll. The strongest memories were waiting for Bess to get home after she'd been with Vince. And when we finally did get together, that night Vince was killed and we made love, it wasn't the passion of first love. Bess's need for me was born out of her grief and what happened between us was a caring, tender act of profound comforting. But eventually, patiently, she moved beyond her grief and there was something close to passion, although probably more for me than for her, and through the years Bess and I were able to know joy and delight in each other.

The dream I had about Molly was vivid. We were on Baker's beach. It was a starry night and I brought the buttery yellow, silky sheets and the blue comforter from the guest room to the beach. We walked for a while and then placed the bedding away from the tide line, back close to the edge of the beach where the trees began. We lay down and held each other. For a long time we stayed in each other's arms looking up at the stars, and then slowly, with exquisite care we found the surprise and excitement of learning about a new body. The way we fit together was thrilling. It was like we were made for each other. And afterwards we lay in each other's arms, only to be surprised again because it wasn't long before we'd make love all over again. When Molly and I were finally almost asleep, I slipped to her side, pulled the sheet and comforter to my chin and closed my eyes. Sleep came and it was peaceful and sweet. But no matter how much I wanted that sweet sleep, I couldn't make it last because fear and an unspeakable dread had swept over me. I turned to make sure she was still there and when I saw her, she was bald and I knew it was from chemo. Ghostly pale, her gray skin hung dull and lifeless on a bony skeleton. And coming down the beach toward us were the same medics who had come for Woody and they stood over us holding a gurney.

It was a terrible dream; it made me feel awful and I woke up hoping I'd be able get it out of my mind. The sun was just coming up and I went to the bathroom and showered, washing my hair and then staying under the spray for a long time as if the water could wash out my brain.

It was just a dream, George.

I know.

You just have to forget it.

I'm trying, Bess.

It will help if you focus on something that needs doing.

Like what? The business is about to be kaput.

You could check on the chickens.

They never meant as much to me as they did to you.

I know. But take a few minutes to watch them.

Go out and watch chickens?

Their lives are simple. It'll help bring you into reality.

Maybe I don't like reality.

It's amazing when you think about how they lay eggs for us.

Eddie's been getting the eggs.

I always felt grateful for them. It might help your perspective, George.

I knew she wouldn't put up with my whining about a stupid dream anymore, so I got dressed, put coffee on and went out to see about the chickens. I checked the feed dispenser to see if it needed filling and checked on the water. Eddie had been taking the eggs over to Lottie's, so I didn't bother with that. I focused on each chicken, carefully noticing the color of their feathers, their beaks and their feet. I've been told that in China chicken feet are a great delicacy and I wonder how anyone could eat them. They look repulsive to me, but I guess each to his own. I had to admit it was different just to look at them, because I'd never actually done that before. Bess knew each one and insisted they had personalities. There was one that seemed to be squawking more than the others. Maybe it was an extrovert. A more verbal chicken. Sort of like Eddie.

While I was watching them, Molly came up the steps from the basement room. She looked fresh and lovely and smiled when she saw me. "Morning, George."

"Hi." I went to the house and opened the door for her. "Sleep okay? Coffee should be ready."

"I'd love a cup," she said, as she came into the kitchen. "And I slept great. It's so quiet here, I could get addicted to this place."

"It can have that effect, I guess." I poured coffee for us, handed her a cup, but I didn't join her at the table. I just leaned against the refrigerator. Against my back, it was like there was a very slight and gradual shift and the refrigerator, instead of being just a refrigerator, began to feel different, like a metal locker lining the wall of a high school hallway. I stared at Molly. I knew I should offer her toast and jam like I had the last time, so I got the bread, jam, a knife and a plate and set them on the counter next to the toaster.

"You know I'd love to go back to the forest where we let the mouse go. What a beautiful place with all those trails." Molly sipped her coffee and looked up at me.

"Island Center Forest. But, I–I can't go—my friend Martha Jane is having some kind of a plumbing problem and I said I'd help her."

"Do you know when you'd be back? I'd be happy to wait."

"I have no idea what the problem is, so it could take hours. You never know."

"Oh, well in that case—since I have to leave this afternoon, I'll go by myself."

"Sorry."

"Not a problem," she smiled, and if she was disappointed she didn't show it.

"Look, I better get going," I said, pointing to the counter. "I put the bread and jam out, and the toaster's there so just help yourself." I took my cup to the sink and walked quickly to the door. Grabbing my jacket from the hook, I turned and waved. "Bye, Molly. If I don't see you before you have to leave—have a safe trip home."

"Thanks, George. Hope you get the plumbing fixed," she said, sounding cheery enough I thought.

"Hope so." I felt stuck by the door for minute, but then I turned and left.

I took the truck down to Martha Jane's. I could have walked, but since my tools were in the back of my truck, I thought it would look like a more serious commitment. At the end of the drive I was about to cross the road to Baker's Beach when I saw Eddie's truck coming down Lottie's drive. He waved and pulled over next to me and put down his window.

"George, I gotta talk to you."

"Now?"

"Not now. I'm heading to Tahlequah to get the ferry. I'm stocking up on some stuff at Costco for Lottie. But how 'bout tonight? Will you be there?"

"Of course. Where would I go? You're the one who's never home." I couldn't believe it, I sounded like a nagging spouse.

"I'll see you tonight then." He waved, put up the window and turned out of the drive.

I drove down Baker Beach Road and noticed there were some potholes between Howie and Mark's place and Martha Jane's. Bess thinks I should have work to focus on. Maybe I could help Martha Jane and get some gravel and fill the potholes. But then I remembered that when I tried to get a bag for our driveway when we were getting ready to open Bluebell Nook, both the hardware stores were out of it. Small bags of gravel must be very popular. And if they still were, I'd have to get it in bulk and by the cubic yard, and that would mean a big pile and then where would I put it? I wouldn't need that much to fill the potholes, so there'd be a big pile of leftover gravel sitting around and it couldn't go in the front yard, it would look bad, and in the road it would block where people parked and they'd get mad. Better to forget it. It was not a good idea.

I hadn't seen Martha Jane since Woody's memorial and as I was coming up the stairs, she opened the door. "George, I heard you drive up. Come on in. I've been wondering when you might stop by."

"I guess it has been a little while." I hugged her and she was so small and round and soft, I thought it might be like hugging a penguin. Although I remembered that was a snarky name for nuns and Martha Jane was a very secular person; if she had been a nun, she'd be like those Nuns on the Bus that rode around the country for social justice. I kissed the top of her head and followed her into the kitchen.

"Tea? The water is still hot."

"You sit down, I'll get it." The mug that Bess had given her was sitting on the counter. The one that said, ALL YOU REALLY NEED ARE BOOKS AND CATS. "Same kind? Orange spice?"

"Yes, thanks. I'm a creature of habit."

"Me, too."

Maria was in her lap when I brought the tea. The kitchen seemed especially cozy—the little table and its blue and white checked table cloth, the small copper pot filled with dried flowers, the yellow walls and bright white trim—it made me feel brighter.

"How are things going, George?"

"Okay, I guess."

"You hadn't seemed quite yourself when we came back here after our service for Woody." Martha Jane cupped her hands around the mug as if trying to warm them. I wondered if she was cold. I've heard that old people get cold, that's why they sometimes keep their houses so hot. Although Martha Jane's house wasn't hot. Old people! What about me? Like I'm some young dude? Jeez.

I dunked my tea bag up and down. "I know I did leave a little early. I guess I have to admit that it was kind of a depressing conversation, about suicide, you know. Everyone wondering if that was how he died."

"I suppose so. But we all need to comfort each other, isn't that it? That's all we've got really. Ourselves and one another. That's everything."

The window over the sink was open and I could smell the sea, there was the scent of salt and seaweed. I looked out at the beach and it must have been slack tide because the water seemed very still. "Didn't you mention you were having a problem with your sink?"

"My sink?"

"Some kind of plumbing problem?"

"Oh, let's see. That was quite a while back, at least a month, and Howie fixed it for me. It was clogged where the pipe bends around to go into the wall. He took it apart and got rid of the gunk that was clogging it and it was all fine." She looked puzzled. "Had I asked you about it? You know I forget things."

"Not really. I told someone I came here to fix plumbing."

"What's going on, George dear?" She reached over and patted my arm.

"Bluebell Nook isn't going that well. The last guest we had, before the one we have now, freaked out because there was a commotion in the middle of the night and something killed a chicken and left it by the door where she was sleeping—the guest room door."

"Oh my."

"It was all bloody."

"I suppose she didn't want to come back."

"No, and again we had to pay so she wouldn't write a bad review, besides refunding her money."

"Did you find out what killed the chicken?"

"No, it was probably a coyote." Then I told her about Eddie's paintball gun and how he shot Lottie's dog with it.

"That does sound challenging. Trying to keep the business going with those kinds of problems, George. But you said you do have a guest now, is that right?"

I nodded.

"Is that going any better?" she asked.

"Maybe."

"There haven't been any problems with mice like the first guest?"

"She doesn't mind mice."

"George, you don't seem like yourself, are you okay?"

"I kissed her."

"The guest?"

I nodded.

"Are you worried she'll write a bad review?" Martha Jane chuckled. "Oh sorry, George. I don't mean to make light of it. But you're not the type to force yourself on anyone, so I'm sure the guest wanted to be kissed."

"I hope you're right." I went to the stove and poured water in my cup. "Would you like more?"

"It's fine, thanks."

I sat across from her and stared out at the beach again. It looked like the tide was beginning to come in. I wondered if Molly had gone to Island Center Forest. I felt stupid, fleeing to Martha Jane's. Maria was purring in her lap and Martha Jane was stroking her. That nice little purring like a low little motor and then moving your hand over the soft fur, rhythmically and slowly—it must be very relaxing. Maybe I should get a cat.

"Martha Jane? You were married twice right?"

"I was."

"How did that work out?"

"The first one didn't work out. We divorced after he came back from serving in the Korean War. We'd married too young and really hadn't been that well suited to each other. You've probably heard what they say about marriage, that the first time you marry for sex, the second time for love, and the third time for money." She laughed. "Probably true fairly often, I think. Anyway, Bernie my second husband died about fifteen years ago. So I've not had the best of luck, although I was incredibly happy the second time."

"Did you ever think you'd want to marry again—after your husband died?"

"A third time? I have enough money." She laughed. "I'm just kidding, George. But I do think widows can do pretty well being single. A lot of us enjoy the freedom, often for the first time in our lives just being able to think mostly about our own needs. Stay in bed all day and read and eat crackers or donuts if that's what we want—you know, that sort of thing. There are lots of exceptions of course, but basically I think a lot of women are socialized—and maybe biologically to some extent, just hard-wired to tune into other people. Women's hearing is better you know, so they can hear an infant at night. That doesn't mean they can't do anything a man can do except pee in the Grand Canyon." She looked puzzled. "Now how did I get off on that? Men peeing?"

"We were talking about widows."

"Oh, right. Thank you. Well, that's it—I think women often aren't in a hurry to give up that freedom, and they often have wonderful close friendships with other women, or are close to children or grandchildren and that can meet a lot of needs for love and closeness. I always liked what Gloria Steinem said, that a woman needs a man like a fish needs a bicycle."

I drank my tea and didn't say anything.

"Oh, dear. I'm sorry George. I didn't mean to upset you. Obviously, lots of men and women need each other. And there are many women who have wonderful, loving marriages. But it's quite different when women don't feel desperate about having to have a man. You can see that, right?"

"I can. I'm not sure I have much to offer anyone,

anyway. So it's a moot point." I got up and took my cup to the sink. "I've got to get going, Martha Jane."

"So soon?"

"Oh I've got a bunch of stuff to get done. But it's always good to see you. Thanks for the tea."

She got up carefully, holding on to the table. Her arthritis often makes it hard for her to get in and out of a chair. Slowly she walked me to the door and we hugged.

"Come back again soon, George. I always love to see you."

I thanked her and waved when I got to my truck. I drove out of Baker's Beach Road, but instead of turning up to my house, I just drove around. I got to Vashon Highway and then I worried Molly might be coming back and she'd see my truck, so I drove over to Maury Island and went down to Pt. Robinson. But then I remembered that she had gone to Pt. Robinson the first time she came to the island. She'd loved it. Maybe after she left Island Center Forest, if she had time before her ferry, she'd want to see it again. Mt. Rainier was out today. It was a beautiful sight from there with the lighthouse and the beach and everything. It seemed very possible she'd want to go there again, so I left. I turned around and headed back to Vashon Highway. From there I turned at Burton and drove west across the island over to Wax Orchard Road. I drove past Camp Sealth until I got to the farm where they had all the goats—the ones that made money clearing brush and eating blackberries. I was glad they weren't out on a job. There must have been around two dozen—all shapes, sizes, and colors. Some with long floppy ears, and some with pointy ears, also some with horns. They were just mellow, hanging out together wandering around the huge yard so I pulled over across the road and I turned off the engine to watch.

AGGIE

MOLLY HAD GONE BY THE TIME I GOT BACK FROM watching the goats. I knew she wanted to avoid rush hour in Portland and had probably gotten the 2:10 ferry. We still had Triscuits and some grapes and cheese, so after I took a nap, I had that for dinner while I watched the Mariners. They were playing the Astros and they were as hopeless as usual. It was only the sixth inning, but I got tired of watching them get clobbered, so I switched if off and I went to the kitchen to get a beer. On my way to the living room I glanced out the front window. The drive was empty. No blue Prius. Why did I think it could be there? That she'd come back? In the living room I sat in the plaid chair and drank my beer and poked the stuffing in the hole in the arm.

I'm making a mess of the chair, Bess.

Don't worry about it.

I don't know what I expected. Especially after I bailed on Island Center Forest.

But you were off to a good start, George.

I don't really know her. And she doesn't really know me.

But she came back a second time.

Maybe she was just lonely.

You're lonely, too, George.

I suppose I'm lonely, too. Lonelier than I knew a person can be. I told you about talking with that phone solicitor.

You've come a long way since then.

But I don't know how to be with somebody.

But you've been trying.

Just because the Airbnb forced me to talk to people.

Talking to people is how you start relationships.

Me and relationships? I know I screwed up not going with her to Island Center Forest. What was I thinking?

You need to remember the three ingredients for a good relationship.

Didn't we go to some event or some program about relationships at a potluck? Maybe at the Burton Lodge? My memory is fuzzy.

We did. It was where couples renewed their marriage

vows. The Unitarians put it on, but it was open to anybody.

I brought fish. A salmon.

The three things are: Number One: Be kind to each other.

Eddie and I caught the salmon. It was September and we were mooching near Pt. Defiance. We had some good fresh herring spinning. It was slack tide and no wind and then my rod started tapping.

Number Two: Laugh together.

The rod bent like it was trying to dive in itself. The reel was screaming—it took out two hundred feet of line. Eddie grabbed me by the back of my pants so I wouldn't go overboard. That fish was the biggest catch of my life. A twenty-eight-pound king. Without Eddie I would have ended up in the drink. If it hadn't been for Eddie …

Do you want to hear the three things, George?

It'll be hard to tell him I'm quitting the business … What three things?

For friendship, any good relationship …

Maybe I should write this down. You used to give me your lists and I'd write things down.

It's easy, George. You'll remember. Number One: Be kind to each other.

Okay. Be kind to each other. Next.

Number Two: Laugh together.

Number Two ... laugh. Okay, got it.

Number Three: Most of all ... forgive each other.

I think forgiveness is over-rated.

You make me laugh, George. You ought to give someone a chance.

I don't know who else would think I'm funny.

You ought to try. I don't want you to be lonely, George.

I have Eddie—even without the business. And Martha Jane.

It's not the same.

I miss holding you, Bess.

Oh, George.

That's where I got stuck.

It's fear that makes people stuck.

The thing I feared most happened—losing you.

And you've survived it.

I'm not afraid to die, you know. I'm afraid of loss.

My mind—my hearing, my sight, my mobility—my independence.

Then choose life. While you still have all that. You've got to turn the corner.

Where have I heard that before?

Give yourself a chance, George.

I finished my beer and took the can to the recycle basket in the kitchen. It was getting full, so I brought it out to the side of the house to the garbage and recycle cans. We have two 32 gallon metal cans for garbage. The metal is to keep the raccoons from getting in the garbage. And we have about a half dozen plastic ones that are same size for the recycle. Plastic is okay because the raccoons don't want to eat the recycle stuff, so they won't chew through it. I actually had wondered if it was a raccoon that killed the chicken, but that woman, the guest—I've blocked out her name—she said the creature she saw running away was big. Some raccoons get pretty big and fat, so maybe. Who knows? The cans were getting pretty full so I'd have to make a run to the dump tomorrow. I actually don't mind going to the dump. I try not to think about landfills and the planet, but just focus on the experience. The transfer station (that's what it's called) is run by the county and it's situated on a beautiful road surrounded by lovely fields that are edged with tall evergreens. So it's aesthetically very pleasing. But I also like the process of throwing the stuff out. Lifting up the cans and flinging all the contents into the huge recycle trailers. And then driving around to where the garbage goes and getting up into the bed of the truck and heaving all the garbage from the cans into the pit. It's very satisfying. You take these full cans and then when you're done you bring them back empty. I like that.

As I was taking the recycle basket back to the house, Eddie drove up. He parked next to my truck and hopped out. "Is this a good time to have our little meeting, George?"

"What meeting?"

"Just us. Like I said, we should talk."

"Okay, fire away."

"Not here. In the house." Eddie went in and went straight to the kitchen. He opened the refrigerator and got a beer. "Want one?"

"Just had one—oh, why not."

"Here." Eddie handed me a beer and we both went in the living room. When I sat down it looked like even more stuffing was coming out of the hole in the arm of the plaid chair. Eddie sat across from me on the couch and leaned forward with his hands on his knees. "So George, I checked the email yesterday and there weren't any bookings."

"Big surprise." I took a big glug of my beer.

"Let me just check to make sure." Eddie jumped up and went to the computer. I braced myself for his next scheme. My house is paid off, and I could just see him trying to convince me to get a loan with the house as collateral so we could add a swimming pool and a tennis court, or a merry-go-round to attract people with kids. And have Scottie come with a dozen bagpipers for a photo shoot for a glossy marketing brochure that advertised an exclusive selection of the finest 25-year-old Chivas Regal and Glenlivet. Actually, thinking about that scotch made me wish I was drinking some and not my can of Bud. Eddie came back and sat down again.

"So, were there any?" I asked.

"Nope." Eddie folded his arms across his chest. "That's what we have to talk about."

"Whatever."

"See, I think the word is out and it's not good."

"You think those people cheated?" I was bracing myself for his next scheme. But as soon as he proposed it, I'd tell him I was done. I had the itemized list of all the money we were losing ready in case he needed any convincing. And I could explain that not having any reviews was almost as bad as crappy reviews.

"What? Who cheated?" Eddie looked confused.

"The guests. The ones we paid not to write bad reviews. Maybe they went ahead and wrote not to come to here. Said it was terrible."

"George, the reality is we paid them not to write bad reviews. But there wasn't a gag rule or anything—"

"Bluebell Nook made them gag." I laughed.

"It's not funny."

"Okay, okay. So we didn't pay them to keep their mouths shut. Just not to write bad things."

"And that's exactly the point. Nothing is more important to a business than word of mouth. And in our case, word of bad-mouth. Those people were pretty pissed off."

"If you ask me they overreacted. Molly was cool about

the mice." I poked the stuffing in the hole of the chair arm. "You know, Eddie—you sure haven't been around much lately. I don't even hear you come in at night."

"Actually, Lottie and I are getting along pretty good."

"Glad to hear that." And I was. Eddie had put on a little weight. He was a lot less scraggly looking from when he first showed up after Marlene had made him leave the attic. And he seemed more relaxed, less jumpy and nervous. It was good to see that.

"Max has really taken to me. Lottie's got arthritis in her knees and sometimes her back gets bad so she can't walk too far, so I take Max for long walks every day and that makes Lottie happy."

"So she's over being mad at you."

"Definitely. And that's part of why I wanted to talk about the business."

"You mean the fact that we have no customers, and we're in the hole."

Eddie put his beer down and sat forward. "Let's face it, George. This isn't working."

I was actually surprised. I'd been bracing myself for another scheme, but it was obvious where this was going, and I couldn't have been more relieved that I didn't have to be the one to do it. But I still couldn't help needling him a little. "What happened to that old never-give-up spirit? You're the guy that always thinks things will work out. Like the Mariners. Every year you believe they'll do great."

"That's true."

"And you read the obituaries and get a lift because your name's not there, Eddie."

"Here's the deal—Lottie wants me to work around her place, help with her Airbnb."

"Be part of her business?"

"Help her out. Not business partners—it's her business." Eddie smiled. "But I'm not exactly only the handyman, dog-walker guy."

When Eddie said that, I wondered if he and Lottie were having sex. I couldn't picture it. I don't know why exactly—the fantasies I'd had about Molly indicated that at my age, I still found the concept very interesting.

"It's like this," he continued, "we'll go to the movies sometimes, share meals. That sort of thing."

"So you're moving in with her?" I asked, wondering if the "that sort of thing" meant he was sleeping with her.

"Not exactly. It's companionship, really."

"That's important, I know." I was happy for Eddie, but to my surprise, since he hadn't been around that much, I realized that I actually felt a little sad, too—because I'd miss the guy.

"She has a room over her garage where I'd be. I hope you're okay with that? With me moving over to Lottie's garage?"

"I think it's a good move for you. And, I'm fine with quitting the business, Eddie. I had come to the same conclusion and was never really cut out for this. Happy Isle Hideaway will work out better for you than Bluebell Nook."

"I had planned to pay you rent. I thought I'd take it out of my share of the profits, but—"

"Don't worry about it, Eddie."

"We never did use that bird book we bought. You can keep it if you want."

"I might fill our old feeder and see who shows up."

"George … thanks." He smiled. "Thanks for letting me stay here."

"You'd do the same for me."

"I would if I had a house."

I put my beer down. "Well, I guess it's about time I get that otter mess cleaned out of my boat. I'm thinking about heading over town to get a new Shimano rod. What do you say we fish on Thursday if the weather's good?"

"You got it!" Eddie went to the kitchen where he put his beer can in the recycle and I walked to the door with him.

"I'll come back tomorrow and get the rest of my stuff."

"Okay. See you Thursday, Eddie."

Before he left, Eddie hesitated for a minute. Then gave me a quick hug.

The next morning after I went out to the chickens and gathered the eggs, I put the coffee on, and while I waited for it I went to the computer. I thought I'd better contact the Airbnb people to let them know that we were going out of business and tell them to take our listing down. I checked the email and then froze when I saw an email with the subject line "Reservation" and the email address—it was from Molly.

Hi George,

I'd love to book your lovely room for a couple of nights this month, Friday the 12th and Saturday the

13th. And, I want to bring Aggie! I know she'll love
Vashon. I'll look forward to hearing from you and
if you're booked that weekend, I'll try to bring her
some other time. Hope this works!

Fingers crossed :)

Molly

I had to reply. I had to figure out what to reply. I
mean, the truth was easy. It was very straightforward.
All I had to do was write her and say that the business
was closed and I was sorry but it wasn't going to work.
It wasn't mysterious. There it was. Matter of fact. Just
the facts, ma'am, like Joe Friday used to say. I always
liked that show. *Dragnet*. The actor Jack Webb wasn't
that good looking, that's probably why I liked him.
And he always solved the crimes. Oh man, here I was
sitting at the computer thinking about old TV shows
instead of replying to Molly and just telling her that
Bluebell Nook was toast.

I don't know what to do, Bess.

Don't worry, George. Bluebell Nook served its purpose.

What purpose? It was a failure.

You weren't.

We just lost money and pissed people off.

Not Molly.

I don't know what to do about Molly since we're quitting the business. Besides, like I told you before. I don't really even know her.

You'll figure it out. I have faith in you.

She wants to bring her dog.

Really.

She showed me a photo. It's a rescue.

That's great—it's really wonderful when you can give a dog like that a home.

It's part Golden Retriever and something else, but mostly it looks like a Golden Retriever.

Oh, they're beautiful dogs.

It looked like a nice dog.

I'm sure it must be.

Bess?

Yes?

I think I might like to get to know that dog.

I think that's a good idea, George.

You do?

I do.

Bess?

I'm here.

I can't always hear you.

I know. But I'm here.

You are?

I'm part of you. I'll always be here.

You will?

I will. And George … that's going to be one lucky dog.

Then I got hungry again and I went to the kitchen and scrounged around for something to eat. Eddie had left some macaroni and cheese from the Thriftway deli, so I had that. I warmed it in the microwave and then ate in front of the TV while I watched cable news. The anchor of the show was Nicole Wallace. She has a very nice smile. I like her show a lot. After I finished eating I got a stapler from the desk and went to the plaid chair. I poked all the stuffing back in the hole and then I squished the fabric together and stapled it. It looked dumb. But it was better than the stuffing coming out. Although I don't think Molly had ever noticed it and if she had, I don't think the fact that it looked stupid would be something she'd even think twice about. After I got the chair fixed—if you could call it that, I went to the computer.

Hi Molly,

Eddie and I decided to close Bluebell Nook. I think it's for the best. But I'd like to invite you to come on the weekend of the 12th. And Aggie, too. I'd like to get to know your dog.

I wasn't sure how to sign it, so I just copied hers.

Fingers crossed :)

George

I didn't hesitate. I hit "send." I just did it. JUST DO IT! I did it! And Molly replied right away—she sent an email with two emoji's—one was a smile face and the other was a thumbs up!

I went to the kitchen and looked around for bowls that would work for Aggie's food and water. I found a couple that would do: a very nice red bowl with a purple stripe around the rim, and a metal bowl that was a little dented, but I thought it would be okay.

Then I checked the weather on my phone. It looked like all the rest of the week would be clear. That was great because it would be easier than cleaning out my boat in the rain. Besides a scrub brush, I might have to take a trowel to get rid of all the otter crap. It had been stuck on there for so long it was going to be a big job. It might take more than a few hours, but it would be good to get the boat cleaned up. I was looking forward to fishing with Eddie on Thursday. We might even catch something.

ACKNOWLEDGMENTS

This novel was written during the first years of the Covid-19 pandemic. Throughout those many months (years!) of limited social interactions, there were a number of friends to whom I am grateful for providing me with a constant and sustaining presence. In spite of the fact that our connection was through email, phone, or virtual (thank you Eric Yuan for founding Zoom) they provided me with a reliable anchor through such unknown and uncertain times. Among them, in addition to my heart sisters, Margy Heldring and Rosetta Moore, were members of the Bookshop Memoir Group: Lynne Ameling, Colleen Brooks, Alix Clarke, Cherry Champagne, Tom Craighead, Michael Monteleone, Jane Neubauer, Kathy Olsen, Trudy Rosemarin, Jessika Satori, Arlene Schade, Barbara Wells, and Cynthia Zant. And also on Zoom, Dan Klein and Faith Reeves helped keep our book group going, a group my husband Joe and I had been part of for over twenty years.

For their contributions and help in bringing this book into the world, I'd like to thank Barry Foster and his (and Bruce's) chickens, Mike Horswill, Jane Neubauer, Lana Protzeller, Masha Shubin, Sandy Trammell and especially with love and gratitude to Amy Kirkman for her wonderful edits and expertise.

ABOUT THE AUTHOR

Jeanie Okimoto (Jean Davies Okimoto) is an author and playwright whose books and short stories have been translated into Japanese, Italian, Chinese, Danish, Korean, German, French, Turkish and Hebrew. Her awards include *Smithsonian* Notable Book, the American Library Association Best Book for Young Adults, the International Reading Association Reader's Choice Award, the Parent's Choice Award, the Green Earth Book Award, and the Washington State Book Award. Her picture book *Blumpoe the Grumpoe Meets Arnold the Cat* was adapted by Shelley Duvall for the HBO and Showtime television series *Bedtime Stories.* She has appeared on the Today Show, the CBS Morning Show, The Oprah Winfrey Show, and CNN. Her short stories have appeared in Dell's anthologies *Short Stories*

by Outstanding Writers for Young Adults; and she has had plays produced in Seattle, Toronto, Vancouver, New York, and on Vashon Island, Washington. Her publishers include HarperCollins, Houghton Mifflin Harcourt, Tor, Scholastic, and Little, Brown. Her novels for adults have received recognition through the Eric Hoffer and Next Generation Indie Book Awards. Jeanie and her husband Joe live on Vashon Island. They are blessed with four children, six grandchildren, and two mostly good dogs.